W9-BDF-729

The Zen of Zombie
Better Living Through the Undead

Scott Kenemore

Illustrations by Adam Bozarth

FALL RIVER PRESS

Text copyright © 2007 by Scott Kenemore
Illustrations copyright © 2007 by Adam Bozarth
Design by Adam Bozarth

This 2010 edition published by Fall River Press,
by arrangement with Skyhorse Publishing.

All rights reserved. No part of this publication may be reproduced,
stored in a retrieval system, or transmitted, in any form or by any
means, electronic, mechanical, photocopying, recording, or otherwise, without prior written permission from the publisher.

Fall River Press
122 Fifth Avenue
New York, NY 10011

ISBN: 978-1-4351-2500-1

Printed and bound in China

10 9 8 7 6 5 4 3 2

For C.C. and E.C., who have saved me from zombies and worse

TABLE OF CONTENTS

INTRODUCTION

I feel like such a zombie today.

Don't just stare at me like a zombie.

I feel like I'm just going through life like a zombie.

We've all heard the slurs and stereotypes, but few people stop to consider how much humans have to learn from zombies. What about all the *good* things zombies do?

This book is a guide through the life lessons that can be gleaned from one of the netherworld's most successful creatures: the implacable, untamable zombie.

Whatever your setback or ailment, zombies feel your pain.

Have you ever felt as if other people were smarter than you? Quicker on the uptake?

Zombies feel this way every day.

Have you ever been tongue-tied while those around you knew exactly what to say? (Maybe when you did speak, it came out as nothing more than some guttural croaks and gurgles, and possibly very simple words like "brains?")

Zombies haven't let this stop them.

Do you drool at inappropriate times? Stagger when you walk? Stare unblinkingly at passersby, sometimes for hours on end, unnerving each one of them?

Friend, a zombie knows your pain all too well.

And yet despite being host to not one or two, but *numerous* psycho-physiological setbacks, zombies have done more than simply survive. They have persevered. And you can too.

Historically maligned and stereotyped for their irritating habits (walking into moving traffic, disturbing graveyard landscaping, eating people's brains), zombies can also be valuable guides through life. Few of us have stopped to consider the valuable life lessons that zombies are able to teach us. Until now.

It is no accident that zombies have proved the most adaptable, reliable, and inveterate agents of the netherworld. While they may not look like much on paper (slow-moving, dull-witted, unspeakably ghastly), they have many skills and qualities to envy.

(Here it should be noted that some zombie researchers have posited the existence of zombies who can move quickly, eat things other than human brains, and are capable of more than halting speech. For our purposes here, these will be assumed to be aberrations rather than the norm. While articulate, omnivore zombies who can win the hundred-yard dash would be interesting subjects to study, it is all the more remarkable that it is **not** these super-zombies who have been so prominent and successful. Rather, it has been the stupefied, outrun-able, dullard zombie—with the most limited and selective of menus—whom we have come to regard as the dominant netherworld force. It is telling that these slower zombies have succeeded despite—or perhaps **because of**—these so called "setbacks.")

Never in history have so many, possessed with so little, done so much to further their purposes as have zombies.

Believe me, dear reader, I was once like you. I used to be a confused, embittered lost soul who haunted the self-help section of my local bookstore. In bestselling tome after tome, I failed to find the improvement I desired. (The smiling, attractive authors on the book jackets seem to have everything that I wanted for myself, but when I followed their prescriptions I was met only with frustration.)

I attended motivational seminars featuring enthusiastic speakers who held questionable credentials and doctorates from horrible correspondence schools, but never did I feel "excited about my life." I hired uncertified and unlicensed "life coaches" to steer me on my way, but they only took my checks and steered me to a place where I still sucked.

I tried motivational tapes and CDs recorded by Zen masters in recording studios on mountaintops. I watched interactive meditation DVDs hand-crafted in Tibet.

Still, nirvana eluded me.

And even as good heath, physical attractiveness, emotional satisfaction, and spiritual oneness were denied me, I saw, in my day-to-day life, many people who had evidently achieved some (if not **all**) of these things I so desired. My first inclination (it was a reasonable one, though misguided) was to attempt to model myself after **these** people. If I could carefully observe them and do what they did, then surely (I thought) I would become like them. More importantly, I would find the common thread—the universal connection between them.

And yet, try as I did, I was never successful in this task. I struggled to see what it was that allowed these exceptional human specimens to become so. I failed, utterly, to find the emulation or patterning that would allow me to take on their characteristics. It seemed like an unsolvable mystery. A club I could never join. A secret society into which I was not invited.

This line of thought only encouraged me to assume that I was a born loser. That from the start, I had been doomed to a life of mediocrity and banality.

Then, one day, I did find it.

I **did** discover that one central, singular thread of synchronicity linking enlightened, successful, and attractive people.

What let them command attention wherever they went and whatever they did? When they spoke, what made others hang on each word? How did they find the temerity to be brave and unflinching in every situation? What kept them from ever giving up? What kept them moving forward?

It could only be . . . that they emulated a creature no less or greater than a member of the walking dead. That is, a zombie.

Once I understood this, new doors opened to me that had been heretofore shut. New experiences came my way, and I found myself granted access to secrets I had never dared dream I would know. Being like a zombie allowed me to attain a **Zen state**. I actualized the reality of my existence, in ways that only the reanimated can. I became the person I had always wanted to be . . . by becoming like a zombie. In fact, the **more** like a zombie I acted, the **better** a person I became.

And you can too.

"But this is so counterintuitive," you say?

Certainly. But hey, give it a shot. Other, traditional self-help manuals haven't solved your problems have they? (If they have, then what're you doing with this book? . . . that's what I thought, you lonely fatso.) The point is, you've **tried** the other self-help books. You've **seen** where those approaches to "contentment" and "enlightenment" lead. You've spent your hard-earned dollars on regimens emphasizing positivity and inner peace, only to find yourself a "negative-Nellie" who's always at war with himself (or herself).

And **since** you've tried the rest, why **not** try the brain eating, grave-opening, speech-slurring best?

Want to be a "killer" in business? Or a lady-killer? Then model yourself after an actual killer for once.

If you want to be the kind of tough guy who says "I eat people like you for lunch" to his enemies, then act like a zombie (who actually **does** eat his enemies—or anyone, really—for lunch).

Being like a zombie is great. When you wake up in the morning, you can do whatever you want. You have no boss. You have no deadlines that you, yourself, don't impose. Most importantly, you have no worries or cares. (Whoever heard of an anxious zombie, right?)

Other self-improvement manuals claim that they want to help you achieve "love" in your life, but ask yourself honestly—would you rather be loved or feared? Zombies are some of the most feared beings around, and their lives are pretty damn good. Being loved isn't everything. Moving less in a touchy-feely direction and more in an eating-someone's-brain direction can have tremendously positive impacts on your self-esteem and sense of existential well-being. You just have to know how to get started.

The first section of this manual contains a point-by-point analysis of the 24 habits, tendencies, and characteristics that make zombies so effective at everything that they do. This section illustrates the benefits of being more like a zombie, and covers the many different ways these benefits can be obtained. Adopt just one or two of these habits at first, if you like. Take them for a test-drive. Go at your own pace. There's no reason for me to hard-sell adopting all of the traits at once, because I'm confident that that's **exactly** what you'll want to do after you've noticed how well they work.

The second section of this manual is a 12-week workshop intended for those desiring a more comprehensive and complete guide to becoming as close to a zombie as you can get without actually being a reanimated corpse (maybe you will be one day, though, if you play your cards right). This section is an intensive zombie-education program that will take you 90 days to complete. It has been carefully designed to provide the most optimal transformative immersion possible. Wish your life could be a "do over?" Want to make a "fresh start" for yourself? This program was designed for you.

Before beginning, ask yourself these questions honestly:

• Am I man (or woman) enough to do what it takes to get what I want?

• Am I ready for a program of self-improvement that will be nothing like the programs of instruction I may have tried before? (And I mean **nothing . . .**)

• Am I prepared to say good-bye to the "old me" so I might be reborn (as if from a newly opened grave) as a dynamic, self-actualized, spiritually fulfilled zombie?

If your answers to these questions are yes, get ready to re-animate yourself for success with secrets from the undead!

PART ONE:
The 24 Habits of Highly Effective Zombies

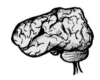

It is obvious to any close observer that zombies have benefited from a combination of carefully cultivated habits and tendencies in order to become the superior specimens they are today. By identifying and emulating these habits, humans can enjoy many of the successes that zombies do.

Zombies don't worry. Not about themselves. Not about others. Not about climate change. Nothing.

Zombies have "enough" of what they need in life (with the exception of living brains). Yet are, at the same time, "driven" with a passion and intensity that any CEO or motivational speaker would envy. Zombies don't stop. Zombies don't rest. And yet, zombies are at peace with this ceaselessness. And you can be too.

Zombies have moved beyond the pressures of society. A zombie never feels it "ought" to do something. A zombie never feels that it "should" be doing something (or avoiding something else). A zombie simply is who he or she is, and is at peace with that fact.

When you adopt the habits of a zombie, it's like a fast track to the effectiveness you seek and the self-actualization you've always yearned for. Being like a zombie cuts right through the treacle of life. Cuts right down to the heart of the matter. (Then, when that heart has stopped beating, it has the brain for supper.)

If you want to become a better person and improve your life, you need to start taking on the habits of zombies.

Habit

1

Be Adaptable

Life's gonna throw you some curveballs, and nobody knows this better than a zombie.

You may have to move far away from home to go to the college or university of your choice. Your company might downsize you around the holidays when you least expect it. Your desiccating corpse might be reanimated by an evil warlock's spell, a secret government nerve agent, or radiation from a UFO.

Life's going to throw stuff like this your way now and then. Need some advice on how to get through it? Look no further than our friend the zombie.

Zombies don't ask "Why did this happen to me?" They don't meditate on the *meaning* of their reanimation. Nope. It's up out of the grave and right on the hunt for brains.

Zombies have a way of making the best of a situation.

Throw a zombie in the middle of the ocean, and hey, it'll get back to land eventually. But in the meantime, it's going to fuck up some sharks, probably an octopus or two, and, damn-straight, any unlucky fisherman it gets its rotting hands on. Sure, one day its inherent drive to locate and consume thinking human brains will drive the zombie back to land—and yeah, it might be down to bone and rags by then, but that thought's not stopping it for a second.

Freeze a zombie in an arctic ice floe. Sure, it's trapped for the short term. The moment global warming reaches it, though—boing!—it springs up good as new, ready to mess you up.

Zombie Tip:

In some languages, the word for "crisis" is also the word for "opportunity."

In the language of a zombie, however, the word for "crisis" is also the word for "a decided lack of yummy humans to eat." (The zombie word for "opportunity" is likewise synonymous with "a school bus full of defenseless children," "a group of overconfident, naïve explorers," and "a crowded country house with the road washed out and the phone lines disconnected from a storm." . . . but you probably could've guessed that.)

Burn a zombie. Throw acid on a zombie. All I can say is that you better finish the job, because those sons of bitches will just keep on coming.

Cut off a zombie's limbs (one by one, if you like) and it will continue to drag itself after you.

See, the zombie doesn't draw the inference polite society might expect it to draw. It doesn't think: "Gee, I'm on fire. I should really stop to put this out before continuing on my way." It doesn't think: "I have no arms and legs left, and inching myself along with my neck is really taking a while. Maybe I should just give up and let the other zombies have all the fun." No! You're not going to convince a zombie it's time to give up and start pouting. It's just not done. (Or not something done by zombies, anyway.) A zombie stops only when its own brain is destroyed or disconnected from the spinal cord. Only under similar circumstances should you consider giving up on yourself as an acceptable option.

Remember to think of the adaptable zombie when life throws **you** something you weren't expecting. It doesn't have to be a villager planting a flaming pitchfork in your chest, or a machine-gun assault by a top-secret federal anti-zombie agency. It can be an irritating foot fracture, being passed over for a promotion at work, or having your car repossessed. Sure, zombies don't (usually) drive, but it isn't difficult to guess what a zombie would do in that situation.

He'd shuffle right to the bus stop, and go to work all the same. And once at work, he would eat the head of his boss (despite an irritating foot fracture).

Habit

2

Play to Your Strengths
(and Ignore Your Weaknesses)

Everybody has different strengths and weaknesses.

If there's a lesson to be taken from this fact, it's "use what you got." It's a lesson nobody's learned better than a zombie.

The luckiest zombies are those with the good fortune to be reanimated directly after mortal life has departed from the body. These zombies, usually still wearing the clothes they were buried in (which, in the case of female zombies, almost always includes pearls and a hat), have the fortune to be mistaken for living humans. Occasionally, these lucky zombies are even mistaken for the *particular* living people they were before they died. The advantages of this are diverse and considerable. A zombie who appears to be simply a drunken or similarly incapacitated human being of sallow complexion has a much greater chance of gaining access to the places where living humans (and their correspondingly delicious brains) are to be found. Some of these highest-

16

functioning zombies are even lucky enough to remember a word or two of human speech. (Usually these will be simple words and phrases like "hello," "yes," "no," and "I am, in fact, a neurosurgeon. Now please let me closer to that succulent frontal lobe.") These zombies are the millionaires, the professional athletes, the rock stars of the zombie world.

But as long as they remain appropriately humble, we have little reason to begrudge them their success. (Zombies are not covetous of one another's good fortune. This is yet another trait we could stand to adopt from them.)

Other zombies (perhaps the majority fall into this category) are lucky enough to have all of their limbs and features, but cannot pass for living human beings. These zombies have deathly pale skin. Their grave-clothes are often generations old. Their fingernails and teeth are long and ragged. Their hair is unkempt and encrusted with soil. Still, these zombies are able to be mistaken for living humans at great distances or in the dark, and often use this fact to their advantage. These zombies can sometimes blend into crowds of inebriated people (such as at sporting events or rock concerts), and can pass unnoticed through inhabited areas on dark, rainy nights.

Other zombies still are less lucky, yet manage as best they can. Zombies in this category are often missing arms or legs. Eyes, noses, and teeth are questionable. Baldness is common. Decomposition, to some degree, has already set in. These zombies are often

---

Zombie Tip:
A brain in the hand is worth two behind the hastily improvised zombie barricades.

Count your blessings, man. When something good comes your way, go ahead and enjoy it. Don't forsake it in favor of what might be behind the next door. Cause it could be some kind of anti-zombie nerve gas the government has been working on, and then you're just fucked.

called the most hideous because they still possess some visible similarity to a living human, but with the most jarring variations thereupon. These zombies induce fainting, vomiting, and the invocation of deities on sight. Tragically, they must exist in a world not designed for them—a world of staircases made for people with two legs, ladders for those with two arms, and voice-recognition software that is hard enough for a living human to use and damn-near impossible for a zombie's rotted vocal cords to operate. These zombies can't pass for human, and don't try to. They win by paralyzing victims with fear. By being a glorious abattoir-on-parade. If someone faints at the sight of them, so much the easier. If a zombie's wounds or half-decayed state is knee splittingly hilarious, then hey, keep laughing while the zombie gets that much closer, funny guy. Maybe these zombies don't look much like people anymore, but the point is, you're still getting eaten.

Any questions?

A final category of zombie may fairly be called the Most Decomposed Zombie. Some researchers have even wondered if these creations ought to count as "zombies" at all. Here you find the walking skeleton, no more than rags, tendons, and bright white bone glistening in the moonlight. Here you find the gelatinous humanoid mass, muddily rising from a grave in the bottom of a swamp and lurching toward land caked in leaves and vines. Here the brain, spinal cord, and gibbering skull, squirming along like a fish out of water. These zombies are not just un-human, but un-zombie-like as well. But fuck it, right? They're still coming for you, and that's the important thing. In fact, maybe that's their advantage. These zombies aren't trying to look like humans. They're mud creatures, or fish, or skeletons, or fish skeletons. They're not going to let you tell them they're not zombies. You don't "get" to tell them what they can or can't be. They're going to crawl or slither or drag themselves after you, and eat your quick-to-categorize brain before it can exclude them from anything else.

In short, the zombies (in all of their various forms) remind us that to be good at what you do, you don't need to be "normal" by anyone's standards but your own. No matter what hand God, or nature, or various artificial reanimating nerve agents have dealt you, you already have everything you need to effectively achieve your goals and follow your dreams.

Habit

3

I Will Choose Free Will

Don't let anyone, or any*thing*, tell you what to do.

When people pick on zombies by using them in analogies and comparative examples, they usually do so it ways that make zombies sound like automatons or robots that are largely unaware. Incorrect as it is, you'll hear people say things like:

> *"Joe in accounting is such a zombie. He's just going through the motions."*
>
> -or-
>
> *"The prisoners are so beaten down they just stand around the exercise yard like zombies."*
>
> -or-
>
> *"Find out what that guy's weakness is, and we'll use it to turn him into a zombie."*
>
> -or even-
>
> *"I didn't bother leaving the couch today. When the play-offs are on, I'm like a zombie."*

21

The problem with these examples is they mistake a zombie's focus and drive for a kind of mindlessness. The idea that zombies find their existence a restraint or a prison is deeply misguided. In fact, nothing could be more distant from the truth.

Other self-help books love to talk about "breaking the chains" that constrain you, or "setting yourself free" from this or that vice. These books are usually written by dilettantes and dabblers in freedom. If you **truly** want to experience freedom—real, radical freedom—you need to make the zombie your model. They are the freest creatures of all.

Acceptance and acculturation into society involves the relinquishing of certain freedoms. Nothing new here, right? I benefit from my citizenship, but the laws that protect me also restrain me. The police will prevent my enemies from murdering me, but they will also stop me if I want to murder **my** enemies. The government provides roads for me to drive on, but I have to pay taxes to build those roads. Yadda, yadda, yadda.

As other self-help books have previously noted, many people are surprised to find that this acculturation has extended even into their own minds.

Some examples are obvious. As much as I might hate my enemy, I don't actually contemplate killing him. I think to myself "Killing him is not something I can do" because so-

ciety has closed it off to me as an option. But in truth, I can by all means kill my enemy. Nothing physically prevents me from ringing his doorbell, and smacking him over the head with his heaviest lawn ornament as soon as he opens the door. Yet my acculturated brain tells me that this would result in my arrest, incarceration, and possible execution. Because of it, my brain removes it as a "lived" possibility I can actually pursue. While physically I **can** pursue it, I have removed that button from the keyboard of my mind.

Less extreme examples also illustrate the way we eliminate certain options from out list of possibilities.

When your alarm rings (at least on a weekday), you likely just get up and head for the shower, no matter how sleepy, or hungover, or under the weather you might be feeling. Your alarm doesn't physically **force** you to rise (when you would very much prefer to stay in bed). Rather, you rise because you have given your alarm power over you.

And it's not just alarm clocks.

Traffic lights. Work superiors. Court-appointed substance-abuse counselors.

All of these things get an automatic response from us **because it saves time and because it's easier than thinking it through**.

In some cases, we don't even think it through the **first** time. For example: "While it sure doesn't **sound** like going to couples counseling once a week (and paying $50 for the privilege) is going to even begin to save a relationship this codependent and twisted, I told Karen I'd give it a chance. I don't want to fight about it anymore, so I'll just assume that if I reasoned it through, I'd elect to go."

Before long, we're walking fifteen minutes out of our way instead of just cutting straight across a lawn because we automatically give a KEEP OFF THE GRASS sign power over us.

Giving things power over it is **not** something a zombie does.

Of all entities everywhere (be they natural, supernatural, celestial, or something else), zombies may be the most free. With an existentialist flourish to make Jean-Paul Sartre blush, zombies realize they are truly able to do **whatever** they want, **whenever** they want. Zombies have noticed that no one can tell them what to do, and that the only limit on their actions is usually self-imposed.

A human thinks: "Even if I want to, I can't kill my enemy. If I do that I'll be shot at or jailed."

A zombie thinks: "If I want to, I can eat that guy's brain **and** get shot at or jailed."

The impending consequence in this example is much the same for the zombie and the human. The important difference is that the human is so acculturated and constrained that he automatically opts out of what he really wants to do. The radically free zombie keeps everything on the table.

When a human says: "Can I do that?" He usually means something like: "Is this legal? Will I get in trouble? Is it permitted?"

A zombie who wonders if something is possible is concerned only with the physical logistics. A zombie might wonder: "Can I break down this military barrier? Can that fat kid outrun me? Can I get through that doorway with this spear sticking through my chest?"

But **never**: "Will I get in trouble if I break down this door? Will eating that fat kid be in bad taste? Is it a social faux pas to go indoors with a spear?"

Zombie Tip:
Remember that YOU have the power to change the world.

Not in any real, meaningful, geopolitical way, of course. But if you're willing to scale things back just a bit, you'll see that real change is possible when you work on a one-to-one (brain-to-brain) level.

True, completely ignoring laws, conventions, and manners doesn't make zombies any friends. Yet there is no evidence that it makes them more hated and feared than they already are. Would a zombie who took care not to block the box as it crossed an intersection in pursuit of a victim be any less terrifying (or any more deserving of mercy from the well-armed)?

Zombies know they're going to be attacked on sight anyway, so why not do whatever you want, right?

To put it simply, a zombie has discovered that it is possible not to concern oneself with whether something is "allowed," or "legal," or "in good taste." There are many benefits to this. It makes zombies direct and effective, yes. But it also makes their defeat (or successful repulsing) a thing that must be tested each time.

A zombie defeat is never self-imposed.

A human army, for example, will usually surrender or retreat when facing an obviously superior foe. You'll hear telling murmurings along the line, like:

> *"We* **can't** *fight an army that large."*
>   -or-
> *"There's* **no way** *we can try to hold off an army that out-numbers us 20 to 1!"*

-or-

"It's **impossible** *to charge an enemy head-on when they're so well fortified!"*

The one thing these cowardly declamations have in common is that they insinuate a lack of possibility where possiblity clearly exists. If an army really **wanted** to, it could easily engage a large, well-fortified opponent that outnumbered it 20 to 1.

Actually, that's just what zombie armies do.

It has already been noted that a benefit of zombie troops is their ability to fight to the last zombie. While human armies are quick to self-select that as an unacceptable ending to an engagement, zombies are free to say: "You know what? Screw it. I'm still charging. We're outnumbered and encircled and they're offering amnesty to all zombies, but I still get to choose what I want to do, and I choose to go down in a blaze of brain-gnashing glory."

To make one final, but important, distinction, it must be noted that zombies are **not** (alas) invincible, and that should not be inferred from the above.

When a zombie chooses to ignore common sense and charge a medieval warrior-king with a flaming sword, that zombie may well find itself at that king's feet with its head separated from its body. Zombies who choose not to give a sign power over themselves, even when that sign reads DANGER: MINE-FIELD, are no less exploded because of it.

The point is not that zombies' radical freedom allows them to do anything. Instead, it's that zombies don't let others force them to control themselves. If you want a zombie not to walk on the grass, you'll have to pull out a shotgun and blow its head off. Humans might do what you want them to just because you made a KEEP OFF THE GRASS sign, but zombies don't work that way.

Sorry bub, but you better start shootin'.

Habit

4

Succeed as a Corporate Zombie

Perhaps no single aspect of life can take as much from the zombie as that of the working world. White-collar or blue-collar, whatever your occupation, if you want to get ahead in your career, look to our friend the zombie.

Most workers arrive at the job site each day with a set of "skills" that end up doing more harm than good. They "think critically." They have "listening skills." They "keep an open mind" and "seek input from all sources" before making a decision.

And (imagine it!) these same people wonder why they don't get promoted.

Allow me to let you in on a little secret, Mr. Jack-Welch-wannabe . . . The qualities that allow a worker to get ahead in the business world are the same ones that allow a zombie to get a head in an abandoned shopping mall: Focus, drive, and determination.

Whether your goal is to one day give orders from the conference-room table or just to get through another day of mindless repetition on the factory floor, make a zombie your model and you just can't fail!

To see just how turned-around on the subject most people are, let's take a typical fresh-faced management trainee on his first day at work.

He's got an empty briefcase, a brand new $1,000 suit, an Ivy-League MBA, and a head full of the latest corporate synergies, schematics, and business plans.

Know what else he's got? No clue about the real business world.

Nothing personal against our hypothetical hero. He's worked hard up to this point in his life, and tried to do what he thought was best for his career. The problem is, all his store-bought "expertise" isn't going to matter a whit in the real world.

He thinks he knows it all, and that business school has pre-pared him for everything. But answer me these questions:

Which of Milton Friedman's economic theories tell him what to do when an executive vice president asks to him to be part of a junta being organized to push out the aging CEO?

Which treatise on the international costs of vertical integra-tion tells him whether or not he should sleep with his boss in exchange for a promotion?

And how do Muhammad Yunus's analyses of bilateral microfinance initiatives help him know what to do when he sees a way to "bend" the rules (that the government regu-lators will almost certainly fail to notice) that could triple profits by the end of the second quarter?

Do our hero's dilemmas sound familiar? Can you relate? Does this hypothetical businessman remind you of, say . . . **you**?

If it does, don't worry. The first thing to do is relax and take a very deep breath.

Zombies have you covered.

The most important thing they don't teach you in business

school is not to do anything too drastic. Why volunteer to be the team leader with all the accountability, when you can be lost somewhere in the support crew? Why stick your neck out unnecessarily just to get the boss's attention? Remember, attention can be negative, as well as positive.

I'm not saying that to be like a zombie you must do nothing at all. Make **some** decisions, sure. (Just like zombies do.) Take action if you have to, but never hastily or quickly.

As zombies know all too well, there's no reason to sprint, when slow and steady also wins the race.

When you're at a department meeting, the less you say, the better. Simple, zombie-like utterances will usually do. A low grunt of assent or dissent gets the message across just fine. A brief nod or shake of the head is eminently more palatable to those around you than a crisply articulated "Great idea, boss!" or a thoughtfully jargoned "I think we need to control expectations as relates to this request."

Besides making you appear to be a ladder-climbing kiss-ass, saying too much can also get you into trouble. It can betray your true (selfish) motives. Things you say can and will be used against you . . . by your boss and by other people who might want your job.

So follow a zombie's example. There's no need to come out swinging with some complicated business school-ese like: "I'd like to dialogue with you about synergizing to exceed standards on best practices for cranial acquisition" when a simple " . . . braaaains . . . " will do just fine.

In addition to being a world in which silence is golden, the workplace is also frequently described as being a "dog-eat-dog" world. Which is to say, man-eat-man. And with the possible exception of South American cannibal tribes, stranded Uruguayan soccer teams, and AVN Award winners, nobody's got more man-eating experience than a zombie.

Are you looking to be more cold-blooded?

A zombie can help you out with that.

The average Gordon Gekko financial district employee has nothing on a zombie. A zombie can eat his former best friend and business partner and feel nothing. A zombie can "cooperate" and "work" alongside others on a "project" when it suits his purposes, and eight hours later be kicking back with a cranium cocktail, his coworkers' corpses strewn at his feet. Allegiances are temporary (and mostly unintentional) for zombies.

Wall Street types think ice water runs in their veins because they rook grannies out of their pensions or use junk bonds to defraud investment houses.

Whatever, Mr. Tough-Guy.

Your average i-banker wouldn't last a day against a zombie. Wall Street types are fueled by avarice and greed. They want money. They want a yacht, a mistress, and a summer place in the Hamptons. Zombies, on the other hand, play for the love of the game.

Tell me, Mr. i-Banker, how are you going to use your business skills to outwit or outmaneuver something that has no use for money? Something that "works" 24 hours a day (while you're catching Zs in your Park Avenue two-bedroom)? Something that has no use for networking events or "being connected"? (The only connection a zombie cares about is its teeth connecting with your occipital lobe, son.)

If your goal is to obtain the man-eating ruthlessness necessary to succeed in business today, make zombies your model, not Wall Street types. A zombie's ruthlessness, hunger, and (quite literal) cold-bloodedness make it the perfect touchstone. (Also, unlike investment bankers, zombies don't wear too much cologne, invest in trendy bistros that go under in six weeks, or try to bang the intern from Barnard.)

For a final thought on this topic, consider the ancient query: "What is work?"

> **Zombie Tip:**
> **Never put off until tomorrow what you can do today.**
>
> Especially when it involves violent, lawless mayhem and cannibalism. Those brains aren't going to eat themselves. Hop to it, dude.

Is, for example, something still "work" if you enjoy doing it? What about if you would still do it even if you had to take a cut in a pay, or for no pay at all? If some aspect of your life not occurring between nine and five is laborious to you and involves great effort, should it not also count as work as well (despite no employment relationship being formalized)?

This antediluvian riddle can never be solved. It can never be solved because each person must find the answer for him- or herself.

Zombies have found their own answer to this ancient query: They make **no** distinction whatsoever.

You might say that a zombie is "always on." There is never a time when it relaxes from its quest for brains, takes off its shoes and kicks back after a hard day's running amok. Zombies take no coffee breaks, vacations, or early retirements. Whatever a zombie does, it's always doing it.

Not to say that **you** must be like a zombie and be "on" 24 hours a day. Rather, the point is to notice that zombies make no distinction between work and play, or between being on and being off. A zombie is what it is. The way it is right now? That's how it's going to be at 9 a.m. . . . and at 9 p.m. . . . whether it's Monday, Sunday, or Pulaski Day.

And while some zombie researchers have, yes, characterized this way-of-being along the lines of "an unending godless feast of carnage and terror," the properly attuned eye can also see it as "finding a balance in your life."

And really, isn't that what we're all working for?

Habit

5

Slow Down!
(You Move Too Fast)

Most aphorisms in praise of "slowing down" to appreciate this or that aspect of life are written by simpering poets (who encourage stopping "to smell the roses") or by vegetarian folk-singers of questionable mettle. Zombies aren't simpering, and they *certainly* aren't vegetarians, but they **do** move slowly. Moving slowly is not a problem for a zombie. To the contrary, as a zombie proves, there can be distinct advantages to a more ponderous tread.

Did you ever hear of a zombie being nervous, or having high blood pressure (or blood pressure at all)? No. Zombies take it easy. If one human runs away, it's not like there won't be others. Slow and steady wins the race, and this is inherently apparent to a zombie.

People make fun of the somnambulist's stagger that is the marching style of most zombies, but few people think of it as being like a really cool pimp-walk. Pimps are cool, and even when they're in a hurry, they manage to put one foot in

front of the other in trademark style. Evidently, zombies are the pimps of the netherworld, and their gait is inspired by the same confidence that gives a street pimp his style. (This may be something of an oversimplification, but at the same time, bitch better have my brains!!!)

Zombies also use their slow speed as a tactical advantage in many situations. Zombies walk but don't run, so fleeing humans usually understand themselves to have a little time to run away. However, in doing so, these humans reliably make very bad decisions, of which zombies will happily take advantage. For example:

Ack, zombies! We just have time to barricade ourselves inside of an abandoned house and nail all of the doors shut, effectively sealing us in until the zombies catch up.

Ack, zombies! We just have time to run deeper into this abandoned mine (or system of caves), which we can only assume must go on forever.

Ack, zombies! We just have time to run to the other side of this tiny island (instead of, say, fixing our boat), where I'm sure there won't be *more* zombies waiting for us.

In each of these cases, it is the impression zombies give that they can be at least temporarily outrun that leads their victims to make these bad decisions. Time after time, the zombie's victims ironically place themselves in situations where the zombies' lack of quickness will no longer be a factor.

Adopting a zombie's style of movement can have numerous advantages for you as well.

When you move slowly, you're apt to notice more of what's going on around you. You'll be more observant and take a lot more away from the experiences you have.

When you move slowly, you'll also be less likely to miss things or make mistakes because you're rushing to "get something off your plate." You won't gloss over the details. Slowness breeds effectiveness and quality work.

And when you're eating something (like, I dunno, say . . . someone's head), slowing down will really help you savor the tasty goodness of the dish. You wouldn't wolf down a five-course meal at Alain Ducasse, would you? Naw, man. Of course not. You gotta slow down and enjoy every morsel. It may take you longer to finish, but you'll be glad you did!

Moving slowly creates opportunity. You can always speed up if you need to, but once you pass something by, it's usually gone forever. A slow-and-steady zombie keeps his options open. You should consider doing this as well.

If you're a slow-moving type, go ahead and be slow. Let the world adjust to you, not the other way around.

That's what zombies do.

Zombie Tip:
The early bird gets the worm . . .

but when zombies are early to stuff, it generally works against them. Their appearance, groaning noises, and powerful fresh-from-the-grave smell are usually clues to humans to stay away. If you want to be like a zombie, err on the side of being late.

Habit

6

Be Your Own Boss

Zombies don't handle subordinate positions well, and neither should you. Zombies are *especially* bad team players when their would-be-bosses are arrogant types who deserve a grisly comeuppance at the hands of oh, say, zombies.

Woe betide the voodoo priest, medieval warlock, or late nineteenth century scientist who thinks he's going to create a zombie to do his or her bidding! Usually, these persons have the best of intentions, and certainly, the idea may be tempting at the time . . . but trust me, it *never* ends well.

Misguided attempts at creating zombies for personal use usually include one of the following:

The Domestic: In other words, a zombie to help out around the house, possibly to carry out the trash and empty the kitty litter. This "zombutler" frees a mad scientist or shaman up to do more important things. Little do these scientists and shamans know that nothing is more important than zombies, and that the zombies themselves could give a fuck

42

about your other plans. Even though they may look cute in little tuxedos and maid outfits, zombie servants are always a *very bad idea.*

The Love Zombie: Let's say your lover has jilted you one time too many. You, like any other pith-helmeted English explorer who has painstakingly cultivated a good relationship with the local witch doctor, might say to yourself: "Right. If I can't have her in human form, I'll get the next best thing." (By this last statement, you, of course, mean that you'll capture her, take her to the witch doctor, and have him kill and reanimate her as your concubine. Ahh, the innocence of a young love.) By the time you execute your plan, you'll realize that your decomposing paramour somehow isn't her old self, and now only loves you for your mind (brain). Any attempts at a tryst will only end with you getting eaten, and not in a good way. Again, zombies don't work for anybody, and certainly not as decaying courtesans.

The Revenge Zombie: Got an enemy who's bigger and stronger than you? Don't have the guts to face him yourself? Want to have him strangled and all the important parts eaten? Want all the fingerprints and DNA left over to belong to somebody who's *already dead?* Using a zombie sounds like a good plan, right? It might even seem at first like it's going to work. It isn't. Sure, release a zombie in your enemy's bedroom, and your enemy may get eaten. But things won't stop there. Either (A) the zombie will be traced back to you, (B) the zombie will find its way back to you, and eat *you*, or (C) the zombie will eat something (or someone) near and dear to you, leaving you distraught and kneeling on the floor screaming "Not like this . . . *Not like this*!" and possibly contemplating reanimating the dearly departed. (This would be a bad idea. See previous scenario.)

The Zombie Army: What power-hungry despot *hasn't* considered making some sort of deal with the devil in order to command a host of the undead? And sure, a zombie army might look attractive at first. The advantages of zombie soldiers are plentiful. They don't need to be fed, paid, or billeted between battles. They can march all night without stopping. They don't complain about being sent to their almost certain destruction, and they can keep fighting after sustaining injuries that would leave a normal soldier prone and shouting for a medic.

That said, there are important ways in which the zombie army fails to perform essential functions of human armies. Prisoners, for example, are usually eaten by zombie troops before they can reveal to you any useful information about enemy encampments. Tactical withdrawals and disengagements are not usually in the zombie soldier's vocabulary. (Once a zombie smells brains, it's on!) Further, your enemy can usually disengage your zombie army whenever he wants (provided his troops can manage a slow jog), whereas your force will have considerable difficulty in pursuit. Most troubling of all, zombie armies tend not to disband when the military campaign is concluded. Instead, they'll turn on the residents of whatever country or kingdom you've used them to capture, turning the very prize you fought for into a desolate wasteland that only a zombie could love. Then, when there is nobody else left, the zombie army will turn on you. But hey, what did you expect? When you dance with the devil, he always gets to lead. And in this case, he'll lead you right into the middle of a zombie army with nothing else to do.

The important lesson to take here is that a zombie works only for himself (or herself). Sure, a zombie's self-interest may momentarily coincide with your own, but at the end of the day, a zombie looks out for number one. So should you.

Zombie Tip:
Believe in yourself!

Well, maybe not your living, complete and total self . . . but you know that "self" that's left when the soul has exited the body and then that leftover corpse has been stashed to rot for a few years before being supernaturally or scientifically reanimated to walk the earth and eat people's brains? **That** self. Believe in **that**.

Habit

7

Whereof One Cannot Speak . . .

Seriously, no one likes a gossip or a motormouth. People who can't stop prattling on and on about endless trivialities will never get far in life. Zombies, by contrast, get very far precisely *because* they place extreme limits on verbal communication. (That is, if they don't eliminate it altogether.)

While a few zombies are completely silent, most can manage at least a moan. Some know a word or two (like "brains"), and high functioning zombies have been known to utter entire sentences. The important thing is, nobody ever heard of a zombie talking more than was absolutely necessary.

What **is** "necessary" for a zombie?

A fair question. The answer? Brains. As many as possible. And while the average zombie's guttural moan of " . . . braaaaaaaaaains . . . " may be little more than an involuntary declaration of love for what it prizes most in (after)life,

the zombie who *can* manage articulate intentional speech uses it only to further his or her ends. A zombie may:

Impersonate an ambulance dispatcher to order more paramedics when all available ones have been eaten.

Use a small amount of speech with one human to negotiate his way into a situation where there will be additional humans (gaining entrance to a building, etc.).

Use a word or two to operate voice-activated doors or machines, provided this will lead them closer to actual humans.

Utter just enough speech to appear human when appearing to be a zombie would be a disadvantage (i.e., hiding; this is rare behavior, and only the highest-functioning zombies ever do it).

Moan to indicate its presence to an unsuspecting human. (This is usually done to corral quick-moving humans into more manageable locations.)

The important thing to note here is that the speech is a means to an end. There's no: "What's up, dude? How was your day? Eaten anybody good recently?" Forget that noise. A zombie talks *for a reason*, and so should you.

There is, after all, a certain gravitas to the speech of a zombie. Not that it's eloquent or pleasant to the ear. In fact, it is neither of these (and, come to think of it, probably a good example of the opposite).

But when zombies do talk, people listen.

If a zombie opens its mouth, some important stuff is about to go down, that, probably, you should know about.

If you want people to take you seriously when you talk, then make like a zombie and keep your trap shut 99.9 percent of the time. Then, when you **do** talk, they'll listen as if their lives depend on it.

Zombie Tip:
Grunt softly, and carry your own arms should they become detached.

Not that zombies care about being called litterbugs, but you never know when arms might come in handy, you know?

Habit

8

Nobody Likes a Player-Hater

Maybe you're a popular, successful person. Bully for you, right? But being popular and successful doesn't mean you don't have problems.

Especially smack-talk from others who are envious of your success.

As the most popular and successful creatures of the nether-world, zombies know all about this. They've felt the sting-ing barbs of envy from all quarters. But they never let it get them down. When you look at a zombie's cohort of com-petitors (the ones that be hatin' on the zombies), the reasons for their envy become clear. Let's do a quick comparison:

Zombie

At the top of its food chain. What biolo-gists call a "superpredator" (nothing eats it; it eats everything). Implacable. Virtually unstoppable. Never fazed, even by the harshest of environments. Never complains. Never falters. Once it sets its mind on something (like eating brains) nothing's going to dissuade it. Clearly, we have much to learn.

Werewolf

Essentially, a person with an inconvenient medical condition. Turns into a murderous wolf when the moon is full. Often goes to great lengths to conceal who he or she truly is. Lives a life based upon deception. Vulnerable while in human form. Often displays shame, regret, and substantial misgivings about his or her wolfier aspects. Basically, a conflicted neurotic who is dangerous to be around once a month.

Vampire

Gayer than gay. And while scientists tell us that approximately 10 percent of the vampire population should be perfectly okay with this (even finding it "fabulous"), the remaining 90 percent are going to spend their entire afterlives struggling with insecurity about their lack of heterosexual characteristics. They'll need desperately to compensate and "show off" for the opposite sex by turning into bats

and sucking people's blood, which will just make it seem like they're trying too hard—and will lead some to wonder who exactly they're trying to convince (like, I dunno, themselves?). Vampires also have numerous, well-known weaknesses (stakes, garlic, dressing like a flamboyant stagehand). Most importantly, a vampire can only move around at night, making it, at best, half as effective as a zombie. In summary, an insecure fop with numerous limitations.

Mummy

The poor man's zombie, mummies have many of the limitations of zombies, with few of the qualities that make zombies so tactically superior. While mummies are, like zombies, reanimated corpses, their province is usually limited to the inside of tombs. And while a zombie is a flesh-attacking, brain-eating dynamo, going after anything and everything in its way, a mummy is usually concerned only with a handful of explorers who have "defiled a sacred burial urn" or who have been "cursed" by an Egyptian priest. While a zombie is seldom sated, even for a moment, a mummy usually returns to the slumber of the tomb once it has revenged itself upon the offending person or persons. Mummies are limited in scope, and fundamentally lack ambition in their projects.

Ghost

Ghosts are just annoying.

The Bogeyman ("Bogeymen")

What, are we five years old now? Seriously . . .

Despite their obvious superiority, and the corresponding envy of others in their chosen field, zombies carry themselves with a modest dignity. Zombies do not deign to respond to those who would begrudge them their successes. A zombie does not allow himself to be provoked.

A zombie is wise enough to know that just the fact of being a zombie itself is the most powerful rebuff necessary.

 Zombie Tip:
Be a lifelong learner.

Zombies are constantly finding ways to adapt and improve themselves, and you should too. Whether it's becoming more aerodynamic by molting off its skin, teaching itself new ways to cross flaming drawbridges and navigate rows of spikes, or learning to recognize and avoid anti-zombie concussion mines planted by government shock troops, zombies are the very picture of a lifelong commitment to self-improvement and education.

Habit
9

Strength in Numbers

We've all heard that story about the coach who told each of his players to go out to the woods and bring him back a twig. When they did, the coach took the twigs and broke one of them to show the players that individually they were weak and could be broken. Then he bound all the twigs together and showed that he could not break them when they were bound. This illustrated to the players that if they stuck together as a team, they were strong and no one could break them. What they forget to tell you is that later that night, as he slept in his bed, that coach was eaten by zombies. Even so, his story makes a good point about having strength in numbers. It's a point not lost on zombies.

Usually, a zombie's chief asset is that he is one of a number of zombies who are descending upon a certain locale. A zombie tends to be part of a group. Where you find one zombie, you will usually find others. Being part of a horde that can infest a town or village has several advantages, all of which zombies have learned to use.

Let's be honest. Most humans can escape from a single zombie with ease, just by running away. Zombies are slow. Zombies stumble. Stay a few paces ahead of a lone zombie and you're going to be fine.

However, if zombies are suddenly **everywhere,** in every direction, infesting an entire town or a significant portion of a city, then "running away" is almost an impossible task. If you run, you'll just run into more zombies. This realization usually leads humans to the second stage of their reaction to a zombie invasion, which is barricading. As has already been remarked, unbeknownst to the human(s), this works directly to the zombie's advantage.

You almost never hear terrified humans uttering cries of "zombie!" Rather, it is "zom**BIES**" that they fear. A small difference on the page, but a vital one in real life.

A single piranha fish would be unpleasant to encounter, but it is not nearly as alarming as the feeding-frenzy that goes hand-in-hand with a group of piranha fish. Same idea with bees or wasps. The danger is that one has stumbled, not upon one, but into a group of them.

So it is with the zombie.

Humans may cry out in fear when they see *a* ghost. Or *a* vampire. Or *an* abominable snow monster. But *a* zombie? A single, lone zombie? Not so much.

It isn't clear that one zombie necessarily inspires fear in humans. Under some conditions, a single zombie is even regarded with curiosity. It is little more than a puzzling anomaly—something to be captured and possibly studied in a lab. You can run away from a zombie whenever you get bored with it. You can leave a

Zombie Tip:
The group that flays together, stays together.

Make sure you take time to incorporate bond-strengthening activities into your life, whether it's taking the kids to the zoo, having a round of frisbee golf with the bros, or hunting down and consuming frightened villagers. Bonding is important.

zombie unattended and have a good idea of where it will be later based on how fast it moves.

On the other hand, an alarmed cry of "zombies!" instills a deep, creeping fear that the barricades have already been compromised. Zombies in the plural will require something in the area of a very large government/military task force if they are to *begin* to be managed or subdued. "Zombies" implies a contamination that has saturated through an area. It says: "We've got zombies, ladies and gentlemen, right here in River City." It's a befuddled doctor checking his charts again and again because he can't believe what he's seeing. Diagnosis: zombies! The infection is here, all around us. The canary in the coal mine is dead, and nowhere is safe.

Remember:

There's only two things that humans wouldn't want to see more than one of . . . and zombies is *both* of them.

It should be noted that lone zombies *have* been successful in their quests to obtain human brains under certain controlled conditions (being trapped alone in a locked house with one or two potential victims, showing up in an airplane or on a moving train, hunting victims in enclosed places like caves), but this should be regarded as the exception and not the rule.

Habit
10

Remember That Assholes Tend to Get Their Comeuppances
(Frequently, at the Hands of Zombies)

We've all got people we don't like: in-laws, work supervisors, probation officers . . . I'm sure I don't have to tell you, the list goes on and on. You might have fantasies about revenging yourselves on these jerks who make your life so annoying. Don't. Instead, leave it to zombies. They have a way of righting wrongs, and usually with a delightfully satisfying degree of poetic justice.

Like okay, let's say there was a pretty girl in school who was mean to all the ugly girls. Including you. It might be fun to imagine throwing a flask of acid in her face or something similar, but that only leads to litigation. Better advice? Leave it to the zombies, girlfriend. Dollars to doughnuts, before the movie's over, some zombie is going to at least bite off her nose. At *least* her nose, guaranteed. Maybe the whole face, but I'm not promising anything. My point is, zombie attacks are like an act of god. If it happens, it happens. Nobody's fault. And if the pretty girl was chasing you, maybe while chanting "Sarah-has-a-unibrow" over and over again, and you just *happened* to run into a secret labyrinth populated by zombies . . . Well, nobody's saying you did it on purpose, right?

Right . . . ?

Or what if you're an Ivy-League anthropologist who has run afoul of a Haitian voodoo priest? Sure, it hurts when he sticks those pins in that doll he made to look like you (with the cute little cargo pants and the faded Columbia University T-shirt). I know it does, believe me. Those pins hurt. You don't have to tell me. And when he haunts your dreams with visions of your own demise at the hands of unspeakable terrors from the jungle's darkest depths . . . that pretty much sucks too. Don't worry, though. Zombies have your back, bruh. They have a way of showing up just when you're tied to some sort of altar and the voodoo priest is getting ready to do some ritual to your hypnotized girlfriend that involves at least partial nudity. Suddenly, bam! The zombies that same voodoo-priest summoned like way earlier for some reason (that you totally forgot about) come

Zombie Tip: Don't count your chickens before they're hatched . . .

or your zombies before they're fully reanimated. Listen up Mr. Mad-Scientist-Warlock Voodoo-Priest Guy. I'm talking to you. Zombies move at their own pace, and they reanimate when their good and ready. So just be patient and thankful for the corpses that do turn into zombies.

crashing through the walls of the hut, fucking him up and totally saving the day. (Voodoo priests have notoriously tasty brains, so he's damn straight being eaten first, just giving you and your lady-friend time to escape.)

Or maybe you're a talented New England painter, unfairly alienated from the mainstream art community because of your ghastly renderings of monstrous corpse-like entities that surge out of the ground late at night to feed on unsuspecting Bostonians. True, your first impulse might be to re-

buff your critics by producing photographic evidence (from life!) of these creatures and causing a city-wide zombie scare, but there's no need to be so hasty. Experience shows that you can count on zombies to even the score without any prompting on your part. Like the self-important owner of an art gallery who totally trashed your work, saying he just didn't "get" it . . . Remember him? Well he's going to "get" eaten by zombies the night before a big gallery opening for some pretentious painter who's half the artist you are. (And probably, the gallery owner's guts will get splattered on a blank canvas that just happens to be around, making some sort of ironic statement about what passes for art these days.)

So take a lesson. When people get all up in your grill, just let it go man.

A higher power is watching and keeping track of what's going on and who is being a jerk to whom.

And zombies are his messenger.

Habit

11

Winners Don't Use Drugs

And nobody's a bigger winner than a zombie, right?

Zombies have important things to do. Zombies can't be bothered by the allure of narcotics. Besides, most drugs are a bad fit for a zombie's personality. Consider:

Marijuana

Leads to relaxation and stupor. Zombies are already relaxed and stupefied.

LSD/Mushrooms/Psychedelics

Look, a zombie's world is pretty "fucked up" as it is. He's a reanimated corpse on a quest to eat somebody's brain, dragging his deteriorating body through a world filled with hostile entities who attack him on sight. If you need a hit of acid to make that any cooler than it already is, then dude, I just pity you.

Amphetimines/Meth/Cocaine

C'mon, who ever heard of a twitchy, garrulous zombie? (Answer: no one.) I mean, get a zombie on coke and all it's going to do is talk your ear off about how much it likes brains, right? And you knew that already, so what's the damn point? In addition, drugs in this category tend to be appetite suppressants, which is antithetical to the primal cravings zombies feel. Suppressing that hunger would just be wrong.

Opiates/Heroin/Pain Pills

There is not good evidence that zombies feel (or CAN feel) pain. By the same token, the mechanism by which pleasure would be felt from the ingestion of opiates seems, likewise, to be blocked. Until the drug companies cook up something that makes you feel like you're eating a human brain,

 Zombie Tip:
Hunger is the best cook.

A little suspicious the way some people have to "spice things up" to get interested, isn't it? When you're really hungry for something, you don't need it spiced up. It tastes just right as it is. Whether it's a timeworn culinary dish or a timeworn romantic partner (or a living human brain), if you're not interested, the problems likely go too deep to be solved by extra paprika or some Victoria's Secret underwear. On the other side of the coin, when you're hungry for a certain something (like a zombie always is) no "spicing up" is ever necessary.

zombies aren't going to be doctor shopping or stealing prescription pads anytime soon.

Despite the above, you mustn't think of zombies as prudes or teetotalers (and certainly not as uncool nerds—zombies are **cool as hell**). Zombies are all about feeling pleasure, but pleasure, for them, doesn't come in a Ziploc baggie or a balloon up the ass of a drug mule. Zombies know what they want in life (brains), and they just go out and get it. They don't have time for the distractions of narcotics. They're too busy living their dream.

And you should be too.

Note:

It is probably worth mentioning that, *were* they interested, zombies would have considerable difficulty gaining acceptance to the drug culture at large. (The difference between a zombie who is "cool" and a zombie who is not cool is very, *very* hard to tell.)

Bros Before Hos . . .

S'up fellas? Can we talk man to man for a second?

We know that bitches and hos have their place, but we also know just how frequently they can be trouble. Am I right?

Every group of friends has at least one guy who's given up on his dreams in order to settle down at the behest of his significant other.

Pitiful.

We all know that p-whipped dude who might, somewhere inside, still recognize that he'd rather be out with his buddies roaming the night for a strange piece of tail, but who can't even make it out the front door when his girl is anywhere in a twenty mile radius. This man is not who you want to be.

A zombie would never let a woman keep him at home. You don't see zombies doing the shopping, picking the kids up from school, or relaxing in an armchair with a pipe and slippers. Zombies have the urge to wander the open plain. They are driven to be who they are.

Don't try to tie one down ladies, cause it ain't happenin'.

Zombies understand that a dude's place is out with his bros. All for one and one for all. Whether it's hitting the singles bars, attending monster truck pulls, or skulking around abandoned summer camps hoping to feed on the flesh of the living, a guy needs to be with his troops.

And what about sex?

If you're not getting any, why should anybody else? You know good and well what I'm talking about. A celibate zombie loves nothing better than stumbling along a secluded lover's lane, finding the prom queen and the quarterback going at it hot and heavy in the back seat, and breaking that shit up.

Horny people are easy targets for zombies. They're

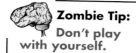

Zombie Tip: Don't play with yourself.

Because playing with other people is so much more fun. Remember, there are no zombie onanists—not out of any sense of guilt or shame, mind you. A zombie would simply rather be out trying to get some* instead of staying home and fantasizing about it.

*brains

distracted, confused, and frequently try to run away with their pants around their ankles, which makes hunting them down that much easier.

It all comes down to being true to yourself. In life, you have to make choices. The zombie chooses never to settle down (or even to stop). Yes, it can seem harsh ladies, but the zombie knows he's got to put his own needs first.

Note:

While it cannot be said that zombies make a concerted effort to consume either sex before the other, plenty of zombies *do* end up picking up girls late at night in secluded places. Especially girls with big, you know . . . brains.

Habit
13

Get the Government
off Our Backs

Zombies aren't known to support one political party or position more than any other, but no zombie will stand for governmental harassment. No zombie likes the idea of the government getting all in the working man's business. A zombie believes honest Americans should be left to go about their lives without undue interference or regulation.

Whether it's a father of four driving a truck to feed his family who can't be bothered to stop at every weigh station, an undocumented worker putting in honest hours for pay that is slightly below the federally mandated minimum wage, or a zombie doing his best to help an orphanage contaminated with children to be entirely rid of them by dawn, the government needs to back off and let these working men and women just do their damn jobs.

State government, federal government, county government—it's all the same to a zombie. That is to say, it's all annoying. Believe me, a zombie knows the pain of having

70

a perfectly delightful romp through an abandoned shopping mall busted up by elite secret service teams with the latest in classified government anti-zombie weaponry. But a zombie **also** knows that a small-town sheriff with a sawed-off shotgun and a hastily assembled posse can be just as problematic. Big or small, the government can get in your way. Whatever the case, the less government, the better in the view of a zombie.

And government regulation!

Don't get me started.

Whenever there's a secret government chemical warfare device that can turn people into zombies, they're always *so* careful about making sure it never leaks out and that nobody is ever, say, accidentally infected. Whatever. Typical government wimpiness! You gotta relax and let that stuff out. Or at least some test monkeys who are already all infected with it.

 **Zombie Tip:**
We have nothing to fear

. . . except the government's eventual, inevitable decision to just say "fuck it" and nuke the entire city we're in. Duck and cover all you like, but when Uncle Sam brings out the nukes, just say your zombie prayers, man, 'cause it's over.

Habit
14

Rugged Individualism

What is the true spirit of an American?

Is it a man traveling alone on the open plain, fueled by nothing but his own gumption and "sticktoitiveness?" Is it self-reliance in the pursuit of your goals? Is it pulling yourself up by your own bootstraps?

Because, if it is, guess what? Boom! Zombies again.

Now sure, there are a few differences between our forefathers' version of the American dream and that of a zombie. The first American settlers wanted a place where they would be free to practice their dumb-ass religions. They wanted not to be taxed by the King of England. They wanted to exploit native peoples and take their stuff. (In some cases, they even wanted to find the "Fountain of Youth.") Later Americans dreamed of luxurious Southern plantations, railroad monopolies, and careers in moving pictures. Today, the American dream seems to involve participation in a reality TV program, saving enough money to pay for gastric-by-pass surgery, and securing an adequately wide audience for one's weblog.

But if we stop to look for the vein of essential "American-ness" running through these pursuits, we come back to self-reliance and rugged individualism.

There's so much to be said for self-reliance.

It's a very important trait. Maybe the **most** important (after, of course, brains). After all, who do you expect to do everything for you?

Your parents?

Ha. They're sending you off to boarding school as soon as you're old enough.

Your so-called "friends?"

They're gonna be out of here as soon as your last credit card is maxed.

"What about Jebus?"

I hear you asking, all suddenly pious-like. Hey kid, everybody knows, Jebus helps those who help themselves!

If you want something, you've gotta go out and get it your-

Zombie Tip:
The universe helps those who help themselves.
Like, to brains and stuff.

self. Zombies are an excellent model for this.

Zombies don't sit around waiting for things to fall in their laps. They go out and get. See, zombies are "doers." And they "do" things like form hideous armies of the night that scour the countryside, eating anybody who gets in their way. They "do" enjoy corralling humans holed up inside of abandoned shopping malls and elevator shafts. They make sure to "do" the things that create environments where humans can get eaten alive.

You never heard of a zombie on the welfare dole, did you? Or some kind of government-subsidized brain-assistance program? Or a zombie who needed help at all?

No.

Think about that for a second. Zombies never ask for help. They don't have to. They help themselves. Zombies find a way.

DIY. That's a zombie, and that should be you, too.

Habit

15

Nobody Likes a Tourist

There are lots of questionable forms of tourism. Sex-tourism. Food-tourism. Even eco-tourism. But no back-packing, pustlegutted, sunscreen-wearing camera-jockey is as offensive as the zombie-tourist. (That is to say, a tourist out to see zombies.)

Say you're a voodoo priest minding your own business in the jungle somewhere. You don't have time for tourists. You got bills to pay. Chickens to cut open and blood to spray all over naked dancing girls. It's a full goddamn day.

Then all of a sudden, these PhDs show up, acting like they're "down" with you. (They're **so** not down.) And after a little introductory chitchat, it comes out that (surprise, surprise) they want you to show them all your voodoo medicine se-crets. At first they'll spin you some story about how they're researching indigenous cures and tropical medicines. Give you a line about how modern scientific medicine is "learn-ing about new cures all the time from native healers and shamans." How the cure for cancer might be waiting inside a plant in the tropics yet unknown to Western science. (But you know better. You went into Port-au-Prince one weekend and saw that movie. It had Sean Connery in it, and it *still* sucked.)

You know why they're **really** there. (It's like, just come out and say it, man.) They want to know about zombies. They want to know how you make them. They want to know what chemicals you use. Then they want to know what plants the chemicals come from, and where those plants grow.

And not for any cool reasons. Not for something you'd be all right with. They don't want to make zombies themselves, or to de-zombify a friend who was accidentally turned into a zombie.

Nope. It's for some boring-ass shit like tenure. They want to write some kind of article about your zombie-making secrets for journals with names like *Nature*. Press them hard enough, and you'll get some namby-pamby bullshit along the lines of "But I'm 40 years old, and I'm still an assistant professor."

Cry me a river, science boy.

Other zombie-tourists are more accidental, but no less annoying. If you're on some kind of expedition through a made-up-sounding country, and a "native" tells you a legend about a prophecy that allows the dead to rise from their graves at such-and-such a time under such-and-such conditions. And you think to yourself, "Hey, those conditions sound a lot like how things are now. What a coincidence! It would be a shame not to take a detour and investigate. . . ." Just let it go man. Things **never** go well for the zombie-tourist in that situation. Even if your native guide is right, and he does give you the right directions to the spot (and not just to an

Zombie Tip:
Your passion shouldn't be a fashion.

If you're just "following the horde" because it's "what everybody is doing," you might seriously want to stop to evaluate your motivations. If you only do what's popular and follow from trend to trend, you'll be left never knowing who you actually are as a person. Who the "real you" is.

(If, however, the horde is comprised of zombies, and you are also a zombie, then by all means proceed.)

abandoned mine where his friends are waiting to rob you), it's not like the zombies who are gonna be popping out of the topsoil are going to pose for photos with you. Think about it.

It has been previously remarked that there is something inherently offensive in the idea of humans going on a tourist expeditions to see other, less civilized humans. Zombies aren't really human anymore, or "civilized" by anybody's standards, but they're still not going to put their rotted, desiccating arms around your Lacoste-clad husband and smile for the cameras. They're just going to eat you. (They're not going to eat you **because** you're an annoying tourist *per se*. They're going to eat you because your brain is delicious. That being said, however, you **are** an annoying tourist.)

Finally, nobody, and I mean **nobody**, has to be reminded of the disaster that befalls the tourist who brings the zombie back as a souvenir. Usually, this will be the explorer type who wants to show off his latest find to his scientist friends. But it won't go according to plan. When he opens the crate that he locked the zombie in, it'll mysteriously be empty. Or else when he puts the zombie on display at some sort of science convention, the thing will get loose and attack everyone in sight. Sometimes the boat that was supposed to have shipped the zombie back will just show up with everyone on board eaten, or turned into zombies themselves, or missing entirely.

So wherever you are and whatever you do, when somebody shows up and starts acting like you're part of some exotic culture worth studying, don't stand for it. Not for a second. Make like a zombie instead.

They won't be back anytime soon if you do.

We're Here! We're Animated Corpses Irresistibly Drawn to Feed on the Flesh of the Living! Get Used to It!

Throughout American history, different groups have had to assert their right to be part of the national fabric of this great country. It hasn't always been easy.

These groups and subgroups have had to fight for their right to exist. To stand up and be counted. To be somebody.

And yet each of these groups has, in its own way, made invaluable contributions to society, science, and the arts. Each one distinct. Each one no more or less American than the other. Yet it has not always been easy for those who at first appeared different in some way.

We love America, warts and all, but sadly zombies cannot hope to be exempt from Americans' initial lack of acceptance for cultures and practices that might appear new and different. We can, however, learn from their perseverance and be inspired by their success.

Zombies are all about breaking down barricades, both the cultural and the very, very literal. If there's one thing zombies know about, it's barricades. And about being left out, and even forcibly excluded.

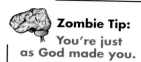 **Zombie Tip:**
You're just as God made you.

Whether you were made to help and inspire others, to forge lasting connections, or to break connections between spinal cords and heads, it's no use trying to change it. It's your nature. (Even if what you do is very, very unnatural.)

You don't have to be an immigrant to be the victim of prejudice. You don't have to have a different skin color or different-looking clothes to be an outsider. You may be descended from people who came over on the Mayflower. You may have attended a fancy prep school and an East Coast college. But even so, something totally beyond your control may drive total strangers to deride and exclude you.

A zombie feels your pain, gay and lesbian America! It's not cool to make fun of someone for their preferences, especially if those preferences have every indication of being innate. Even in this day and age, a lot of people still think zombies "choose" to eat brains. It's like, get a clue. If zombies had any choice in the matter, they'd be eating a steak like everybody else.

Would a gay guy "choose" to like other men, even though he knew it would mean facing a lifetime of intolerance, prejudice, and censored *Sex and the City* reruns on TBS?

A zombie wouldn't "choose" to be a murderous reanimated corpse if he knew it would mean being shot at, exploded, and beheaded whenever someone could manage it. Zombies can't help their preferences any more than you or I. And why should they have to?

Dammit, this is America! And in America, you get to be yourself. Even if it goes against the belief systems of others. Even if it contravenes accepted norms and conventions and laws of nature. And even finally, yes, if it means that you may forfeit your very brain itself.

Who knows? One day, the governor of a northeastern state may even call a press conference to subvert an impending scandal involving clandestine meetings with handsome undead men in hotel rooms, and announce "his truth" that he is a Zombie-American.

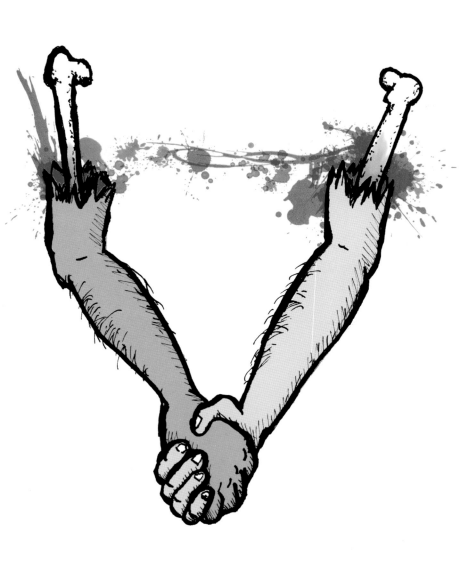

Habit

17

Age Ain't Nothin' But a Number . . .

Victor Hugo once said that 40 is the old age of youth, but that 50 is the youth of old age. Which proves only that Victor Hugo, though an expert on many matters, didn't know balls about being a zombie. Erudite aphoristry aside, age is nothing, and zombies make this clear.

So you're turning 40? Nothing to a zombie.

50? No big deal.

65? Not batting an eyelash.

103? Sure, why not?

Zombies can spend decades, or even centuries, in the sweet embrace of charnel earth before being reanimated. And while they may have been in their twenties or thirties at the time of their terrestrial demises, many zombies are at the century mark when called upon to rise from their graves.

Does that stop them?

Not for a moment.

Zombies never think, "Gee, I'm really getting up there. I should take it easy." Zombies never wonder if they're too old to be at this party and just creeping out all the college girls. And, most importantly, a zombie never says, "I'm getting too old for this stuff." (Because for a zombie, that "stuff" would be terrorizing the living in an eternal quest to sate that which cannot be sated. To quench an unquenchable, atavistic thirst. To chomp as many heads as possible. And ain't no zombie too old for that.)

For most humans, age is relative. To a 14-year-old, 35 seems ancient. Ask 14-year-olds what they hope to accomplish by 35, and the response will be more like "What **won't** I have accomplished by then? I'll have a rocket-car, the awesome house with wall-to-wall speaker systems, and own my own business that inspires magazines to write about how I'm awesome."

Ask a 30-year-old what he or she hopes to accomplish by 35, and you're going to hear stuff that makes you think this person has scaled back expectations just a **teensy** bit. Stuff more like getting enrolled in night school classes, or paying off student loans and trying to scrape enough money together for a down payment on a place somewhere.

Zombies, however, have liberated themselves from this paradox of chronology.

Zombies have advanced, in a very real sense, beyond age. Because their afterlives can pretty much go on indefinitely, the age by which they feel they ought to have accomplished something is almost a nonsensical notion. Importantly for us, it exposes the emptiness of the notion when applied to living humans as well.

Who's to say that someone who's 28 is too old to be living at home, or that by 55 one ought to have started saving something towards retirement?

Such distinctions and notions are meaningless to a zombie, and so should they be to you.

Zombie Tip:
Love you long time.

When you find something rewarding in your life that you truly love doing (mentoring inner-city youth, building houses for the homeless, consuming the still-sentient flesh of the living) make time for it, because man, you gotta have priorities.

Live in the Real World

Most of us know a few poor souls who, for whatever reason, have difficulty dealing with reality. Their "solution" for this, nine times out of ten, is to construct a world of their own that they find more palatable than the real, actual one. This kind of self-delusion could not be farther from the earnest, reality-loving temperament of a zombie.

Don't think zombies aren't tempted to delude themselves from time to time. Believe me, there are plenty of aspects to a zombie's reality that aren't the easiest to cope with. He's an animated corpse with poor motor control and little to no speech driven onward by a desire that is never satisfied. Those who encounter him either flee or attack with all their might. He is "discriminated" against in virtually every way possible.

What's worse, when a zombie's hungry, he can't just go to the grocery store or corner market like you and me. It would be nice for him if he could, but it's just not the case. A zombie has to track down living humans and eat their brains.

Despite all of these middling-to-large inconveniences, no zombie has ever chosen to "escape" from his reality into, say, a world of pills or drugs or booze. No zombies have joined religions that promise a better "next life" in the here-after. You never see zombies joining the SCA or playing role-playing games in which they pretend to be someone else. It might be momentarily tempting, but zombies realize that they have to be where they are. They have to live in the now, regardless of how difficult it might be.

A zombie realizes that the only thing worse than having to

Zombie Tip:
Stay on the lookout.

Think enlightenment will just smack you upside the head one day when you least expect it? Not likely. That's how you get hit by a truck. Whatever you're looking for (spiritual zen, true romantic love, a brain to eat) you've got to be looking for it if you expect to find it. Otherwise . . . bam! A truck. I'm not even kidding.

grow up and live in the real world is what happens to you if you "decide" not to. You'll have to face reality someday. We **all** have to. Running from who you are and where you are will only make it worse when the time comes.

Some humans have living situations that are more or less tolerable, but are haunted by things and occurrences from their pasts. These people may look fine and dandy from all outward appearances, but are tortured inside by things that they did (or things that were done to them). They let these things from the past bring them down and make their lives miserable. This behavior is also unacceptable to a zombie. Zombies have difficult pasts too, but it doesn't stop them from getting on with "life."

Think about it. One moment you're lying there a corpse, minding your own business and enjoying the sweet lethe oblivion of the grave, and the next you've been reanimated by some chemicals you've never even heard of, and your life takes a turn you totally didn't expect. You're walking the earth once again under a pretty daunting set of conditions when you'd much rather be napping away in the dirt. Zombies don't waste their time pining over what might have been, however. They accept their situation and move forward (literally), always making the best of things. Always looking ahead—never backwards. Always searching for the next brain to eat. Always slouching toward the future.

No matter how adverse your current or previous situation, remember these three immutable zombie truths:

You are here.

It is now.

Eating a human brain is the most perfect pleasure imaginable.

Habit
19

No Profiling
(Racial or Otherwise)

Judging people based on how they look isn't cool. Just because somebody looks a certain way, like they're a criminal or something, doesn't mean they are one.

Maybe you've got an armful of tattoos and you like to ride a motorcycle. Fine. That doesn't mean you're in a meth-dealing biker gang, right? You could be a hip orthodontist who just likes cruising with your D-school buddies on the weekends. But the cops will still pull you over before anybody else, perfect teeth or no.

Or what about a guy whose face is dirty and whose many layers of clothing are unwashed and reeking. It doesn't necessarily mean he's a homeless guy. He could be a sociology professor doing research on how homeless guys are treated ... or something. **You** don't know. But PhD or actual urine-soaked bum, when the teenagers start looking for somebody to hog-tie and set on fire, he's number one on the runway.

Not to boast or brag, but bad as some groups might have it, nothing compares to the profiling tribulations suffered by the zombie.

As has been noted, zombies are instantly and mercilessly attacked on sight by law-enforcement personnel. No quarter is given. No Miranda rights are read. The bullets and concussion grenades only stop when the zombie's head is no longer attached to its body.

Old women faint and young women scream at the sight of them. Most everybody without a gun or hacksaw runs away.

If there's another group that gets a worse reaction, I'd like to hear who it is.

As the victims of the worst kind of profiling possible, zombies make sure not to tolerate those who do it.

 Zombie Tip:
"White zombie?" That's just not cool.

Seriously, you wouldn't say "male nurse," "woman president," or "black doctor" (unless you were Arthur Conan Doyle). Why do we need to say what race or sex or color or creed a person (or zombie) is? It's the twenty-first century, for goodness sake. A black doctor can remove your appendix just as well as a white one, and a white zombie can remove your brain just as skillfully as a black one. Damn. Quit being so prejudiced all the time.

After all, just because *some* zombies in the past *might* have tried to eat your brain, doesn't mean you get to automatically assume the next one will, Mr. Prejudiced-Guy. You can't judge one zombie based on the actions of other zombies.

All of this prejudice might get zombies down for a second (they don't show it), but zombies don't let profiling faze them. They say, sure, you might judge me by the way I look at first glance, but that's your loss, because I'm going to impress and surprise you. I am going to defy all your expectations.

You think just because I'm a reanimated corpse that you somehow "know" me. That you can classify me. Put me in a group that you can then write-off. Well don't write me off just yet . . .

Like . . . let me guess. You're probably thinking that you're "safe" from me because you "know" I'm a zombie, and that "means" I'm land-based. It isn't my fault that all the zombies you've seen so far have been on land. (What about all the people who get buried at sea and then become zombies?) Sorry, but your being disabused of this stereotype is going to involve nothing less than my climbing aboard your boat in the middle of the night and eating your brain.

Likewise, if you've securely boarded-up your windows and doors against zombie attack, you might think you "know" that zombies won't also climb up through the sewers or slink down your chimney. But they will. In droves. I pity you, man. You think you're safe, when in truth your problems are just getting started.

Zombies are expectation-defying, stereotype-smashing machines.

The next time prejudiced people with a bunch of preconceived notions act as though they know someing about you just because they know your race or religion, go ahead and surprise them. Be like a zombie.

Habit

20

W.W.Z.D.?

Maybe the person you already model yourself after was a little like a zombie . . .

People get sensitive when you bring Jebus into things, especially things like zombies. The hypothesis that Jebus himself might have been a zombie (and the corresponding religion he founded something like a zombie-cult) is just too radical for most people even to consider. So instead of asserting anything directly, let's just look at some facts and let people make up their own minds:

Everyone agrees that the big J is known to have died, stayed dead for three days, and then to have been magically reanimated to walk the earth once again. That is to say, he rose from the dead.

He was known to raise the dead himself when it suited his purposes.

Jebus wore rags, sandals, and had an unkempt beard.

(Zombies are also known to appear in this fashion.)

Jebus was attacked on sight by the "authorities" of his day, who regarded him as "dangerous" and "a threat to society."

When he was put to death, a "regular" execution simply wouldn't do the trick. It took a "special procedure" to keep him down.

Jebus had a crew of 12 others like him, and they traveled together and worked as a team.

His people stumbled through the desert.

He taught that everyone can be, in a sense, resurrected.

His followers were frequently covered with open wounds and sores.

He could apparently traverse water without drowning.

Jebus was never really in a hurry. He didn't run a lot. Slow and steady won the race, wherever he was going.

The organization founded in his honor maintains blood-drinking and flesh-eating rituals to this day.

Whenever news helicopters float above a city infested with zombies, showing footage of the carnage, people think that these *particular* zombies are representative of *all* zombies. That just because *these* zombies on TV happen to be ransacking the city and eating everyone, that's what *all* zombies everywhere would like to do.

And, of course, it *is* . . . But still . . .

This media bias is not going away anytime soon. The important lesson to take away is how zombies handle this prejudice. Zombies don't let it get them down when the media portrays them in an awful light, or doesn't offer any sort of counterpoint or response to give people the zombie-perspective on something.

Zombies just forge ahead.

You should too.

Habit

22

Remember, It's Just Stuff

Zombies don't focus on material possessions, and they certainly don't "keep up with the Joneses." Neither should you.

After all, nobody likes keeping up with the Joneses. Especially if they have a car or can run fast. As soon as they see you, they're just going to take their tasty craniums and high-tail it right for the bomb shelter. And no matter how fast you stumble after them, it's usually a lost cause (unless one of them has a broken leg or is in a wheelchair or something). Don't worry though, because there's a lesson here. And that lesson is, forget the Joneses, and completely forget trying to keep up with them.

Plenty of self-help gurus throughout the ages have preached about the danger of growing too attached to material possessions. It's a point they drive home, and with very little subtlety. Why? Because for whatever reason, this is an idea that will simply not sink in for most people.

We all must know, deep down on some level, that the trappings of this life amount to nothing in the end. No favorite piece of clothing can give our lives the happy ending we desire. No exotic artifact, no matter how rare or imported, can come with us into the afterlife.

House. Car. Stamp collection. When you go it's just going to get picked over by relatives you never even liked that much.

We've seen it happen to other people.

We know that it's going to happen to us.

And yet . . .

Something deeply instilled in the very core of our beings makes us refuse this obvious truth, that possessions are fleeting and material things cannot last.

What is it about our possessions that cries out: "Hold on to me! Even when it makes no sense to do so. Even when the task of preserving me is time-consuming, expensive, and (at the end of the day) impossible! Hold on to me at all costs!"

Whatever the impulse, it isn't one of our better ones. How can this be known for sure? From the fact that in the most excellent zombie, one finds absolutely no trace of this characteristic whatsoever.

Zombie Tip:
Simplify, simplify, simplify!

Simplicity is key to the freewheeling essence of a zombie. The more things you can eliminate from your routine (like persona, hygiene, clothing, and complete sentences) the better.

A zombie has no respect for possessions, period. Not for its own possessions, and certainly not for things owned by other people. A zombie keeps its goal (brains) foremost in its mind. It doesn't allow itself to get distracted by anything else. A zombie has no difficulty "letting go" of things.

When in pursuit of a victim, a zombie may lose articles of clothing on tree branches or door frames. It may leave one or both of its shoes when it chases someone through a muddy field. Eyeglasses or glass eyes. Tiaras or tube-tops.

Once they're gone, a zombie isn't stopping to pick them up.

Attachment to possessions would only hold a zombie back and would only waste time. Stopping to retrieve a lost shoelace or a treasured childhood knick knack would only distract it that much from its prize (a victim's brain).

You see, a zombie understands that time is valuable, and material possessions are expensive in more than one way.

Here's an example. More than one person has pointed out that if you worked out Bill Gates's compensation to an hourly wage, then he's making something like $50 every two seconds. So, theoretically, if he's on the job and accidentally drops any amount of money less than $50, it's not worth his time to take two seconds out of his workday to pick it up. In that two seconds, he'd make more money by staying on the job.

Think about that . . . Let's say he drops $49. That's a lot of money. You could eat a pretty nice steak dinner for $49. You could do a lot of things with it. And it's not even worth **two seconds** of Gates's time.

It's the same deal with zombies.

Nothing is more valuable to a zombie than eating somebody's brain. Thus, attachment to (and corresponding care of) material possessions doesn't make sense for a zombie (unless, somehow, it brings the zombie closer to that goal).

So when you see a zombie comically lose its top hat while passing through a low doorway, remember that there's a good reason why the zombie doesn't stop to pick it up.

Think back to Bill Gates.

When you see a shabby-looking zombie dragging itself after someone, remember: "**Here's** a guy who's got his priorities straight." Sure, his graveclothes may be missing a few buttons. His hair, fingernails, and teeth (to which he was very attached in life) may now, in the afterlife, have been left behind entirely. His pants may be trailing after him, hanging by a thread and dragging in the mud. But he's not stopping to mess with any of it. He's going right after what he wants.

Material possessions be damned!

It's a resolve that humans could stand to cultivate.

Habit
23

"Live" Free or Die

Throughout history, great men and women have had to struggle against dictators and tyrants who wanted to keep them from living the way these men and women felt they should.

Zombies might not be "alive" or "living" in the traditional sense, but does that mean that they're letting anybody mess with them or keep them down? Hell no.

When the King of England unfairly levied taxes on American colonists, they responded by performing numerous acts of civil disobedience. They tarred and feathered tax collectors. They dressed up like American Indians and threw tea into Boston Harbor. And that was a good start, but nothing compared to what zombies would have done.

In the 1960s, hippie protesters responded to governmental policies they regarded as unfair by burning their draft cards, moving to Canada, and staging three-day outdoor rock concerts. It was, granted, a lot of fun for a lot of people, but zombies were not impressed.

Even in contemporary America, there are some who protest involvement in wars in the Middle East by staging elaborate protest marches on Washington, making celebrity appearances at costly charity events, and by getting the band (when it is Rage Against the Machine) back together. While those involved in the no-blood-for-oil and band-reformation movements are deeply invested in their causes, it will not surprise you to know that in the estimation of a zombie, they are all rank amateurs. Zombies, after all, are the godfathers of civil disobedience. It's hard to think of laws that they **don't** violate:

> *Jaywalking? Check.*
> *Breaking and entering? Big check.*
> *Murder? Check. (However, it should noted that the capacity of zombies to commit first-degree murder varies by jurisdiction. In Texas and Louisiana for example, wanting to eat someone's brain **does** qualify as premeditation.)*
> *Manslaughter? Check. (Zombies can accidentally kill some humans in the course of intentionally trying to kill other humans.)*
> *Destroying property? Big check.*
> *Trespassing? Great big check.*
> *Disturbing the peace? Biggest check of all!*

While a lack of libido does mean that zombies tend not to commit sex crimes (except accidentally), it's still a pretty impressive record. Zombies also don't pay taxes, don't register with Selective Service when they turn 18, and regularly disobey zoning laws. (In the U.S., only the inside of a few secret government labs in the New Mexico desert are zoned for zombies.) And when highest-functioning zombies attempt to operate automobiles, it is almost always with a license that is expired by decades.

But speaking of laws violated, it is important to note that while other groups can violate county law, state law, federal law, or even international law, zombies are that rare class of entity that can also violate natural law. (Note that "natural law" is an umbrella term including the laws of the universe, the laws of science, the laws of reason, religious law, and All That Is Sacred and Good in the Universe.) Zombies have proved this one again and again.

How many times has a shaky rural deputy poured round after round into the chest of an advancing zombie while crying out in disbelief: "Well shoot, sheriff, they just keep on a' comin'! That ain't right."

Consider also the many instances of flummoxed

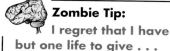

Zombie Tip:
I regret that I have but one life to give . . .

to being a zombie! Seriously, many of our most celebrated patriotic figures who "died" for causes and/or gave up their "lives" for what they believed in, were actually just zombies doing what zombies do. Did you honestly think those people would be getting killed for "ideals" or "what they believe in" or something? Grow up.

medieval warriors who, sword thrust after sword thrust, have remarked to their zombie foes: "Why won't you **stay dead**???"

Don't forget, either, the crafty vacationer, along with her bevy of improbably attractive friends, who has booked a weekend in an exotic tropical resort on the hundred-year anniversary of the great zombie uprising on that particular island. Though her friends are long since eaten, she has managed to shoot, stab, and incinerate (with a Molotov cocktail hastily fashioned from the resort bar) the zombie who has found its way up to her floor of the hotel. And yet, when this zombie, bullet-riddled, knife sticking out of its belly, and still slightly on fire, continues to advance towards her fortification made of overturned room-service carts, our heroine will doubtless scream something along the lines of "Why???" "How???" or that old standard, "What **are** you???"

The answer, of course, is a being not bound by natural law. It is a being that you can stab and shoot and set aflame, but that will not go down unless you destroy the brain or sever the head. It is that outlaw of outlaws, who scoffs at regional, local, and yes, even natural ordinances, regulations, and axioms. And who is coming to eat your brain, like it or not.

In other words, a zombie.

24

Digging a Grave? You've Got It Made!

Most of all, **do what makes you happy.**

That could be the best thing about zombies. They know what they want and they go out and get it. They go in a straight line, right to what they want. Whether it's the path of least resistance or the path of being firebombed by government troops, a zombie takes that path if it leads to tasty brains. A zombie's going to get what it wants, and fuck you if you think you're going to stop it.

Zombie Tip:

A brain by any other name would still taste as sweet.

Medulla oblongata. Occipital lobe. Corpus callosum. Not exactly what you'd associate with the chef's special. But hey, it doesn't matter what you call it if it's what you want!

A zombie doesn't hesitate, and it certainly doesn't doubt itself. No zombie ever says: "I'd really like to give the whole eating-your-brains thing a try, at least for a while. So right now the plan is to move to New York City after graduation and give it a go, but if I don't eat at least one brain by the time I'm, like, thirty, I am *so* totally moving back home and applying to law schools."

A zombie doesn't hedge its bets or give itself timelines. Once it makes a decision, it sticks to it.

It's down for (after)life.

It will pursue its goal to the very ends of the earth.

The rest of us could aspire to such dedication.

PART TWO:
Your Guide to Complete Zombification in 90 Days

Up to this point, we've established not only the unerring dominance of the zombie, but also the many benefits humans can reap from modeling their own behaviors and characteristics after zombies. Certainly, the prospect of this can be intimidating at first. No doubt many readers of this book would not dispute the effectiveness of zombies in a number of (even most) situations, but many might still flinch at the notion of becoming like a zombie themselves.

"I'd like to be more like a zombie," you might say, "but I'm an environmental lawyer from Brockton. Can I really make the zombie transformation? I mean, I take the train in to Boston every day just to get to work. Wouldn't a zombie try to eat everybody on the train or something? This all begins to feel like it might hurt my chances of making partner."

Reasonable concerns, but unfounded. Actualizing your inner zombie will only make your rise to dominance in your profession that much quicker.

"Well what about me?" you say. "I'm a record store manager in Minneapolis. Being like a zombie might give me a lot more hardcore street-cred with the customers, but also, wouldn't I want to eat my customers? And I have enough trouble with employee retention as it is. Is anybody going to want to come to work for a zombie?"

They will.

Work for a zombie. Patronize zombie-owned businesses. Display zombie customer loyalty. It's all there. **Have no fear.**

"One more objection," another says. "I'm a doctor in Denver who just got married and moved to a neighborhood

---

 **Zombie Tip:**
Visualize it!

Visualization is a time-tested self-help tool, especially for zombies. Zombies can "see" themselves tucking into a nice head (most especially when that's what they're doing, right then, at that very instant).

with good schools. Zombies are interesting from a medical standpoint, but I'm concerned that my association with them could damage the credibility and relationships I've worked so hard to cultivate since starting my practice."

Yeah, doc, it might. But you've got to give being a zombie a chance.

This section of the book will outline a week-by-week plan for actualizing your inner zombie in just 90 days. That might seem like a long time, but think about it: Real zombies actually have to be dead, sometimes for years and years, before they start getting the maximum being-a-zombie benefit.

Count yourself lucky, chief.

Week
-1

The Preparation

In the week leading up to the start of your zombification, you'll want to get your affairs in order. Not like some who's going to die . . . or rather, not *exactly* like someone who's going to die.

That's sort of the point.

In the week before starting this program, you'll probably want to put your most valuable possessions into storage . . . anything you wouldn't want smashed or trampled. Imagine, for a second, a zombie bouncing around like a lost pinball inside your trendy bachelor apartment or cute little single-girl condo. What would get broken, or smeared with goo, or partially eaten? Ask yourself these questions seriously, because that zombie pinball is going to be you. Also, mail forwarding? A good idea. Automatic bill-pay on your computer? Set it up, brother. That is, if you want the lights left on.

Pets that can forage (dogs, cats) will probably be okay, but if you've got a bird in a cage or something, it might be time to let Mr. Budgie spread his wings and soar off the edge of the building. You're going to have more important things to think about in the coming months than birdseed and fresh newspapers. ***Most importantly***, ask yourself if you can really make this 12-week commitment. Be honest with yourself.

Zombification is challenging enough when the conditions are right and your dedication is a hundred percent. Advancing only part-way towards becoming a zombie is very dangerous. Zombie-conditioning is hard to reverse. You could find yourself presenting a PowerPoint one moment, and screaming for brains the next. If you go in with any doubts or conflicts, the chances of your finishing are small indeed. Which is a problem.

The lessons in the early weeks will get you started down the right road, but a little knowledge is a very dangerous thing. Make like a zombie in the wrong time and place, and the fallout can be catastrophic, fatal, and extremely unpleasant. (You'll notice you've never heard of a "semi-zombie" walking around, or a guy who was "a little bit zombie now and then." That's because they don't last long, those types.)

Finally, you must tell no one what you plan to do. It can take you right out of the zombie frame of mind to have nice Mrs. Perez from across the hall popping over to see "how the zombie project is going."

At the other extreme, you don't want an enemy of yours to get wind and use this as an excuse to call in the social workers and have you taken away (or, failing that, calling in a military air strike). Your condo association showing up with torches is also a bummer.

But more than any of this, you want the effect of your zombification to be that of a striking transformation. It's one thing to see someone become gradually more like a zombie over the course of weeks. It's even better when you don't see them for three months and then run into them at a social function after complete zombification. That way, there won't be any of that "Gee, you've changed a little" or "Something about you is different . . . No, wait. Don't tell me."

Instead, it'll be more like "Holy fuckface mother of shit!!! Bill, you're a **zombie** now???" And you can be all suave and play it off like "Oh, yeah, I guess you're right. I almost hadn't noticed."

Zombies don't do it for the attention, or the fame, or the free concussion grenades, or any of the other things that come their way. They do it because it's the right thing to do, and the one truth path that they inherently understand they must follow. Are you ready for this kind of dedication?

Now's the time to find out.

No Fear? Know Fear!

Our first week's exercise is all about fear. What you're afraid of, and what you're not afraid of. And, oh yes, who fears you . . .

Zombies enjoy the best possible combination of these factors. They fear nothing, and everything fears them (everything sensible, at least). But let's back up for a second. Sure, seeing the dead rise from their graves to gorge on the living brains of a graveyard caretaker is scary. But it's not the only scary thing out there. Job interviews are scary. Credit card bills are scary. Third dates are scary (like if you're thinking maybe you get to have sex, because its the third date and all, but then maybe it's crass to just assume that you do, but then maybe she's expecting you to try something and if you don't make a move you'll come off as some kind of "half-man." So what's it gonna be? Is that what you are, then? A half-man?)

A zombie is scary, but it's just one of a lot of scary things you have to deal with from day to day.

Now what if I told you that instead of *feeling* fear (at a job interview, at the opening of your bank statement, or in a midtown bistro you can't really afford) you could i*nspire* fear? Things might be a little different then, right? Sure they would. And mostly in a good way. Mostly . . .

At the start of Week 1, make a list of everything that scares you or makes you feel fear. It can be long or short, very detailed or very general, but it should look something like this:

THINGS I'M AFRAID OF:

Stray dogs
Dealing with my ex-wife/ex-husband
Big hairy spiders
The grocer with the scar who works at the meat counter
Death
Taxes
Credit card fees
Grade school gym teacher
Learning a foreign language
Ninja throwing stars
Being seen in my underclothes by even a small group of
    people in good lighting
That one mannequin in the window by my bus stop (al-
    ways stares at me! wtf???)
Using too much curry when I cook and ruining a meal
Third dates

Now, and this may be a bit of a stretch for some readers, make a list of everything that fears you. It doesn't need to be (and considering the demographic who tends to read self-help books, probably **won't** be) very extensive. It could look something like this:

THINGS THAT FEAR ME:
Attractive members of the opposite sex
Very small insects (not counting spiders!)
Particles of dust on the day I do the cleaning

All done? Good.

So, as you sit there feeling superior to a particle of dust, I want you to hold up both lists and compare them. One is a lot longer than the other. Why is that? Well, you're human, after all. (A situation we'll work to remedy as soon as is practicable.) It's in your best interest, genetically speaking, to keep the things it's wise to be afraid of foremost in your mind. Those who don't do this are liable to try petting tigers to see if they're friendly and so forth. (These types are not

Zombie Tip:
Nothing ventured, no brains gained.

A zombie takes chances, and so should you. You're not going to get anywhere in life being timid all the time. You got to have some guts and get out there. (You wuss.) Make like a zombie and charge that policeman. Take on that pitchfork-wielding mob. Take a chance! Live!
. . . in a manner of speaking.

usually around long enough to pass along their tiger-petting techniques on to subsequent generations.)

As for your shorter list, you may have not yet paused to consider the benefits of being feared.

When we talk about "being feared" or "inspiring fear in others," there are several similar activities from which we must distinguish ourselves. Activities and projects that, as zombies, we are most certainly *not* engaging in. These include bullying, gangstering, and threatening. Allow me to explain.

Bullies, unlike zombies, are fundamentally insecure. They want to be powerful and esteemed, but their insecurity requires them to create situations where they can forcibly affirm these things constantly. A bully on the playground steals milk money, not because he really needs the extra 70 cents, but to remind everybody (most of all, himself) that he can take it. That he is bigger and stronger, etc. The bully at work forces his entire staff to work late just to prove that he is powerful enough to do it, not because there is any pressing deadline to be met. This behavior is very unlike a zombie. A zombie never distended a victim's jaw while chiding "Why're you eating yourself? Why're you eating yourself?" Zombies don't do things because they need a burst of confidence, or because they want their superiority affirmed. They just want your brain, and you're right to fear them only because they're actually coming to get it.

Like zombies, gangsters also inspire fear, but zombies aren't gangsters. Whether it's the Al Capones of a bygone era or the Tupac Chopras of today, gangsters are all about building a rep and using it to build an empire, usually a criminal one. It's all about money. People fear gangsters because gangsters will kill to get what they want, and will seriously mess with you if you somehow interfere with their bootlegging/drug dealing/energy drink-endorsing enterprises. Stay out of a gangster's way, however, and he may be nice to you, or even help you out. Zombies, on the other hand, have no secondary interests needing protection. A gangster says "You'd better not mess with me 'cause I'll fucking kill you . . . though under the right circumstances I could be your friend." A zombie says "You'd better not mess with me 'cause I'll eat your brain if you do. Then again, I'm going to eat your brain anyway, so whatever." Gangsters are violent because they have interests to protect. Zombies are just being themselves.

Finally, some humans (many, in fact) use fear to threaten people. There is an if/then-style proposition to it all. **If** you don't let me ride your bike, **then** I'll break your arm. **If** you don't take me fly fishing, **then** I'll cry the whole way home. **If** you don't give me that promotion, **then** I'll sleep with you. There is no "if/then" in the brain of a zombie. Zombies will kill you and eat you no matter what you do. If you let me ride your bike, then I'll eat your brain. Going fishing? Getting eaten. Not going fishing? Still getting eaten. Are we seeing a pattern here? The thing to take away is that zombies don't leverage the threat of eating someone's brain against something else. What they want is the only thing they want.

Contrary to these other types, the fear inspired by a zombie is not the fear of a bully, a gangster, or somebody making a threat. The fear inspired by zombies is, in contrast, the purest kind of fear. It's like the fear of a bolt of lightning or of a hungry tiger. It is the fear of things that cannot (or will not) be reasoned with. The fear of something with no ulterior motive. It's something with no ego to flatter or hidden agenda to uphold. No amount of digging into its past will unearth a secret about a bolt of lightning that you can use to keep yourself safe from it.

Okay, so let's hold up our lists and notice once more that one is strikingly more substantial than the other. Now, for a moment, imagine this scenario, however radical it may seem at first: What if everything on your THINGS I'M AFRAID OF list were magically transported to your THINGS THAT FEAR ME list?

Suspend disbelief for a second and drink that feeling in.

Feels good, doesn't it? That's how a zombie feels every day. And your 90-day zombification can make it possible.

Consider this:

THINGS THAT FEAR ME *NOW THAT I'M A ZOMBIE:*

Stray dogs (Animals are instinctively terrified of the walking dead. If they bark when you walk by, it is only in terror.)

Your ex-wife/ex-husband (Not going to go within miles of a zombie, much less stop by to collect alimony payments.)

Big hairy spiders (If you're a zombie, you might have a couple of these guys crawling around inside your head anyway.)

The grocer with the scar who works at the meat counter (Want a second scar, tough guy?)

Death (Zombies are already dead.)

Taxes (Zombies don't pay 'em.)

Credit card fees (Zombification voids credit card contracts.)

*Grade school gym teacher (No, **you** take a lap. Hard to do without your brain, isn't it?)*

Learning a foreign language (Zombies only need to know a few words, which makes a foreign language vocabulary that much easier. It's "le brain," right?)

Ninja throwing stars (Easily removed from a zombie.)

Being seen in my underclothes by even a small group of people in good lighting (Being a zombie has a leveling-out effect on personal attractiveness. You can have a six-pack or a big ole gut, but when maggots and big hairy spiders start crawling out of your belly, nobody's going to remember which it was.)

That one mannequin in the window by my bus stop (Mannequins are easily destroyed, even by slow-moving zombies.)

Using too much curry when I cook and ruining a meal (Brains taste better raw.)

Third dates (Hey baby, ready for some hot, teeth-on-brain action?)

Zombies succeed because they make the conscious (or unconscious) choice not to have fear. This is not always because a zombie has absolutely nothing to fear. Rare as they are, it has been demonstrated that some things can kill or stop zombies. There are special government shock-troops with anti-zombie grenades. There are magical enchanted swords that can slit a zombie nave to chops and then cut his head clean off. There are zombie-reversing nerve reagents that can send zombies back into the slumber of death from whence they came.

These are real, legitimate fears for a zombie. But look, a zombie doesn't just sit at home with the blinds drawn worrying about it. He doesn't peer cautiously around every corner as he advances, wondering if there's an enchanted magic sword waiting to decapitate him.

A zombie doesn't let worry stop him, or even slow him down. A zombie sallies forth, inveterate.

For your first week of zombie training, you will work on cultivating a zombie-like fear persona by practicing fear-inspiring exercises. These occur when a situation arises in your day-to-day life in which you feel fear. It can arise from any of the things on your THINGS I'M AFRAID OF list, or it can be something else entirely, as long as it makes you feel fear.

When fear occurs, follow these easy steps:

1. Fear (I am feeling fear/I feel afraid right now)
2. Source (What is the source of this fear-feeling?/Why am I afraid?/What am I afraid of?)
3. Reversal of Fear (What would it take to reverse this situation such that the thing that is making me feel afraid would, instead, be afraid of me?)
4. Implementation (Make it so)

For example, let's say you're on your way home from work one evening when a shady-looking character waves you over. You hesitate. Could he have something to tell you? Could he be a good Samaritan with a message? A long-lost relative, waiting to give you a hug and write you into his or her will? Could he be a beggar, just wanting some change? Could he be a mugger who's going to lure you into an alley and stick a knife in your ribs?

**You have no idea.
But you know you feel fear.**

Step 1 is Identification of Fear. So you've already done that. You know you feel afraid. (See how easy this is?)

Step 2 is Identification of Source. Shady looking fellow.

Step 3 is Reversal of Fear. What would it take to reverse the situation? Or, more accurately, what would a zombie do. You've got to think like a zombie here. Maybe you turn the tables and beckon this guy over in a disturbing or menacing way. Maybe you screw your face up into a weird expression that's only three-fifths civilized. (Or three-fifths living.) A zombie wouldn't be fazed by any of that crazy-guy energy that you can tell is pulsing underneath his coffee-stained overcoat and collared shirt from Goodwill. A zombie would show no fear.

So you've got some ideas here. The fourth step is easy, just to make it so. Make is so like a **zombie**. You can be like: "Hey, crazy-looking guy . . . No, *you* come the fuck over *here*. How about that? What does my menacing, drooling expression indicate? What ought you to take from the fact that I desire, earnestly and deeply, to bite your face off? Good questions! Step just a little closer and I'll show you! Just a little closer . . . "

At first you may have to pause and think about each step in turn when fear accosts you. After a few days, however, it should become second nature to turn around the fear and project it back on the fear-originating thing.

Like, Hey, stray dog. You sure jumped out at me all sudden-like, and you look as though you'd certainly like to break through that fence and get at me. Maybe you feel like that fence protects you, and you can just bark at people all day without actually having to tussle with any. Well, I'm the guy who's going to call your bluff. I'm the guy who's going to open the latch and then get down on all fours slobbering and biting you back. See how you like it.

Scary credit card bill? You sure arrived quicker than I thought you would, and with all these surprise penalties tacked on for good measure. Very impressive. How about this? I'm going to put you in a safe place, like the trash, and then sit down at my computer and create my own bill which I'll send to your return address in Delaware or South Dakota. In it, I'll detail the "penalties" I intend to impose for any future correspondence from you. Many of which, interestingly enough, involve eating your brain. (It should be noted that zombies aren't known for their credit scores. However, they rarely have any difficulty obtaining things they want, and are excellent negotiators.)

Keep a Fear Journal during this first week in which you chronicle each instance of feeling afraid and turning the fear around. And don't worry if it's not always successful at first. Write down the failures as well as the successes. Failures can be valuable when you go back and look at why they didn't work.

One past participant in the 90-Day Zombification program (let's call her "Sally") found that keeping a Fear Journal allowed her to refine her successes and analyze her mistakes. For example, one of Sally's failures was chronicled in the following entry excerpted here:

Fear Journal Day Three – This morning my boss Mr. Smith stopped by my desk and started talking about how there are going to have to be some layoffs around the office to meet budget, and said that my work hadn't exactly been stellar as of late. Right away, I started to feel afraid. I didn't want to lose my job. I also didn't want to work hard. It was quite a conundrum. I thought about the steps I was supposed to follow. How was I supposed to turn this around on Mr. Smith? I had to think quickly. "Mr. Smith," I said, "I'm feeling afraid that you won't take me to dinner tonight." It was all I could think to say. And sure, it worked, but it wasn't the zombie solution. Anyway, in the throes of passion later that night, I realized what I should have said: "Smith, you ignorant fat philanderer, firing me would cost you your own job by the time you got through with the sexual harassment and employment discrimination lawsuits. And I hope you like working hard, because even if you succeed in getting rid of me, you'll have weeks and weeks of depositions and meetings first. Wouldn't it be a lot easier if we both just went back to playing Minesweeper?" That's what I'll say next time this happens.

Sally is currently a top-level executive at an investment banking firm in Manhattan.

Your own Fear Journal should contain both positive and negative experiences. The important thing is to learn from both your successes and your mistakes. The ultimate goal is that a zombie reaction to fear should become second nature.

Remember:

To feel fear is unlike a zombie.

To inspire fear is very like a zombie.

You are, day by day, becoming more like a zombie.

Week
2

Sticking to Your (Zombie) Guns

We all have things we want in life. Zombies want to eat living brains, sure. But you probably also want things, too. And they don't have to involve brain-eating (although, if they do, we're not here to judge, obviously). You might want a new house. You might want a promotion at work. You might want a new husband who doesn't pick his toes at

the dinner table. It's up to you. Whoever you are and whatever your desire, this week we're going to focus on the thing you have in common with a zombie: the wanting.

The zombie's devotion to what it desires is total, all-consuming, even slavish. However, zombies are also effective at what they do and tend to get what they want.

Probably, in your life, you have had to make compromises. ("Compromise" is, of course, not even in the vocabulary of a zombie.) Likely, there have been things you wanted to do, but didn't do because doing so did not seem prudent. It may have seemed dangerous. Fiscally unwise. Likely to result in itchy sores on your privates.

Whatever the case, humans have a way of weighing consequences and frequently deciding against pursuing something that they greatly desire. This is just one way in which humans are inferior to zombies.

A close inspection, however, will reveal that this failure to pursue things we really desire stems from an impulse we have just spent a full week attacking. That is, it stems from fear.

Consider:

> *I'd like to jump off the trestle-bridge with the other kids, but I'm* **afraid** *of hitting my head.*

> *I really want to buy that nice apartment in Wicker Park, but I'm* **afraid** *the adjustable-rate mortgage will bankrupt me in five years.*

> *It'd be awesome to get backstage at this Skid Row reunion tour, but I'm* **afraid** *that if I bang the roadie with the backstage passes around his hairy neck I'll wake up tomorrow with something requiring penicillin.*

In all of these cases, we see how fear prevents humans from going after what they really want with the gumption and alacrity of a zombie.

At this point, we should be well on our way to defeating fear, but fear is not the only thing that prevents humans from a zombie-like pursuit of their goals. Another big one is the C-word: *Compromise.*

Humans have a way of getting talked out of things, often things they really want. Frequently, the person talking them out of what they want to do is themselves.

Did you ever hear of a zombie being swindled? Or losing his nerve? Or being talked out of something?

No you didn't, because it doesn't happen.

Humans are talked out of things all the time. More accurately, humans *let* themselves get talked out of things all the time. Humans compromise. Humans settle.

> *I'd like to jump off the trestle-bridge with the other kids, but my dad says it's dangerous. Maybe if I jump in from the bank it'll still be sorta fun.*

> *I'd sure like to get a place in Wicker Park, but the realtor says he's got a place in West Garfield Park that's almost as nice and a little more in my price range.*

> *I'd sure like to get backstage and meet Sebastian Bach, but banging that roadie with all the passes looks scary. The drum tech says I can have some free drumsticks though, if I just give him an HJ in the tour bus. Maybe I'll do that instead.*

Typical humans . . . putting off what they really want because someone has talked them out of it. Someone has led them to a sensible compromise. Someone has helped them make a prudent, safe move that minimizes their risks.

Who makes compromises? Well, you don't. Not anymore. Realize that when someone asks you to compromise, they are negotiating with you. *You do this for me, and I'll do that for you*, and so on.

Zombies don't negotiate.

Neither should you.

Take a typical zombie situation where negotiation could occur (some would say it obviously ought to occur), and watch how it doesn't. Say a bunch of zombies have a group of terrified humans trapped inside a remote farmhouse. The humans might have a couple of small arms and some garden implements, and the zombies have, well, other zombies. It's a standoff. Any police negotiator will tell you that the two sides are at an impasse. One wants in, the other wants out (and to get a county or two away, just for good measure). Right now you're just taking pot-shots at one another. Now and then the humans get brave enough to wing one of the zombies, but that's pretty much it. Again, a conflict resolution professional will say that the only thing that "makes sense" in such a situation is to begin a dialogue. To "get the two sides talking" and so forth.

This is exactly what the zombies **don't** do.

Could you imagine how silly a zombie would look negotiating? How would that even work? "You send out that one guy with the really big head and the rest of you can go." But what's sillier than a zombie trying to negotiate? Trying to negotiate *with a zombie.*

Just as you never see zombies trying to talk their way into something, you never see trapped humans trying to talk their captor zombies into a compromise. Zombies don't negotiate because they're ambitious. What they want is to eat your brain, and they're not going to settle for less than that. Unless you're willing to part with your brain, bub, then you better keep reloading that shotgun and nailing shut those doors.

Remember:

It makes no sense to negotiate with zombies. This is obvious to everybody.

In connection to the above, your lesson for week two will involve cultivating a zombie-like tenacity to get what you want. As the Boss says: no retreat and no surrender. But also, no fucking negotiating with these sons of bitches. Whatever you want, whether it's seconds in the lunch line, a Lexus in the driveway, or a higher spot on an organ recipient wait-list (or, again, to eat someone's brain), you need to make sure you are sated only by the acquisition of the thing you truly desire. And not anything less.

The first exercise, to be completed at the beginning of the week, is to make a list of recent compromises you have made. This can be any sort of situation in which you set out to get one thing, but ended up with anything less. The list needn't be excessively extensive, but should include your original goal and then what you settled on. For example:

RECENT COMPROMISES I HAVE MADE:

Went into boss's office to demand a 20K raise. Let him talk me down to 3K and an extra vacation day.

Told single buddy that I wasn't going to spend my whole Saturday night as his wingman just so he could chat up the new girl from shipping and receiving. Ended up talking to "the fat friend" at some after hours bar until 4 a.m.

Told myself that I'd start going to a new dry cleaner if they ruined another shirt. Sure enough, they ripped the buttons off my red shirt. Everybody hates that shirt except me, and it would be a longer walk to go to another dry cleaner, so I'll just let it go. (But the **next** *time they ruin a shirt, I am* **so** *out of there . . .)*

Went to video store to get new Scorsese DVD. All copies were rented. Went home with director's cut of Casino *instead.*

Ordered bacon and sausage pizza. Went to pick it up and they'd made a broccoli and sausage pizza instead. Paid for it anyway.

If you stop and think about it, you should be able to come up with at least a handful of examples like these—times that you didn't get what you wanted and let that be okay with you. (It's that second part we're going to work on presently.)

Now, let's look at our list and try to figure out what would have happened in these same scenarios if we hadn't compromised; if, instead, we had been totally uncompromising. If we had acted . . . like a zombie. There may be more than one possible outcome. Take your time and tease out all of the possible outcomes (within reason). As you do this, make a new list. It could look something like this.

RECENT COMPROMISES REDUX, WITHOUT THE COMPROMISE PART

Went into boss's to demand 20K raise and refused to negotiate or compromise. He eventually gave me the entire amount.

   -or-

He fired me on the spot.

Told single buddy I wouldn't be anybody's wingman until 4 a.m. Made good on threat and left him at the bar, blue balls and all. At home with the wife watching SNL by 11:30.

Dry cleaner ruins my best red shirt. Who cares if nobody else likes the shirt—I like the shirt, okay? And I am not coming back to this dry cleaner even though

I have to forevermore walk all the way over to god-damn Amsterdam Avenue to have something starched. I liked the shirt that much.

Video store doesn't have new DVD I want. Pretend to be one of the people who sensibly called ahead and reserved one. Thus, the DVD is obtained.

They give me broccoli on my pizza. Broccoli on my fucking pizza. What the hell? Who even eats pizza with broccoli on it? No, I'm not paying for this, and yes, I'm taking it anyway. Because I said so, you smelly stoner, that's why.

Feels good, doesn't it? Easier said than done, sure, but being totally uncompromising is an art form. It takes time, but is completely worth mastering (and completely *necessary* to master if you want to be like a zombie).

"Hey, not so fast," I hear you saying. "Things mostly worked out okay in those examples, but what about that first case? That guy might get his raise, but he could also lose his job entirely. What's up with that?" A fair question. Sort of.

Yes, our hypothetical compromiser (and thousands of actual people with dilemmas like his) could be in some trouble if he lost his job. That **is** part of the situation. He also wants a raise, however, and he can't let **fear** of joblessness prevent him from going after what he wants. (If fear is still an issue for you, please repeat the exercises in the last chapter for another week before proceeding.) If our hypothetical hero does get a pink slip for insisting on a raise, then he can always go get another job . . . another job where he makes 20K more than he was making at the first place. The point is, if he's not going to get what he wants (a 20K raise, right fucking now), it's pointless for him to stick around anyway. It makes more sense to go back into the job market and try to get something that will satisfy his salary requirement.

Whether as essential as one's compensation or as trifling as the topping on a pizza, being zombie-like in your utter refusal to compromise has numerous and immediate advantages.

The exercise for the rest of week 2 involves the steady cultivation of a drive **for** the things you want and **against** compromise.

Here's a little thought-experiment to prime your pump.

Imagine a zombie at one end of a football field.

In the opposite end zone is a delicious human, tied to a chair and waiting to be eaten. The zombie will, of course, set off in the direction of the human as fast as she can. Now imagine an enormous sack of money falls from the sky into the zombie's path. Small bills. Non-sequential.

Know what? The zombie's just going to walk around it.

Now, as she gets closer, imagine that a beautiful/handsome person of the sex to which the zombie was formerly attracted supplicates itself at the zombie's rotting feet. While the zombie may stop momentarily to eat this looker's brain if practicable, she will be only momentarily slowed in her advance to the opposite side of the field, and will not be seduced at all.

As she gets even closer, around the 50 yard line say, the zombie confronts a gaggle of endless flatterers. These members of high society tell the zombie that she is the new belle of the ball, and that if she will only leave with them, she'll be whisked off to a world of exotic getaways, glamorous parties, and grainy green-tinted sex tapes. Our inveterate zombie will not bat an eye.

Now, as she nears the opposite end zone, the really big guns come out. In

Zombie Tip:

It is better to die on your feet than live on your knees.

Lots of zombies live on their knees because their feet have simply rotted away, but that's not what we're talking about here. We're talking about submitting to the rule of a foreign power, which zombies would never do. A zombie serves only him- or herself. So should you.

her path are the deeds to most of the real estate bordering Central Park. A mysterious figure taps her shoulder and whispers an invitation to join Skull and Bones. Majority members of the Supreme Court announce that they have concocted a legal maneuver that will allow her to be sworn in forthwith as the first zombie President of the United States.

And **still** our zombie marches forward towards her goal. Never hesitating. Never asking for more information ("Could I eat Kennedy's preserved brain if I was zombie-President?"). Never negotiating. If she's tempted by any of these things (and there is no reason to think she is), she doesn't show it.

She simply walks to the other end of the field and eats her victim's brain. Why? Zombies don't compromise. Zombies don't get distracted or tempted. Zombies **stick to their guns!**

During week 2 of zombification, you will take steps to identify when compromise is occurring, and to combat it as swiftly as possible.

When people or situations attempt to ply you with compromise, follow these three easy steps.

1. Identify that a compromise is in the works.
2. Remind yourself of your original goal in the situation.
3. Redirect the situation toward that goal (and that goal alone).

Journaling may prove useful. (Yesterday's Fear Journal becomes today's Compromise Journal, etc.). As with the previous week's exercise, you will want to record the situation leading up the event, how the event was handled, and (if compromise took place) how it might be better handled in the future. Here's an example:

> *"Compromise Journal Entry #4, Week 2 of Training—Today I got to my job right at nine o'clock, and the elevator was really crowded when I got to it. Carol, one of the nice, older ladies who works in finance, was like, 'I think we're about full-up. Sorry, no more room in this one.' Reminding myself of my zombification training, I quickly understood that a compromise was in progress. I was being asked to wait for the next elevator. Reminding myself of my original goal in the situation (to get on **this** elevator), I quickly took steps to redirect the situation. Forcibly removing Carol from the elevator and replacing her with myself, I achieved my original goal. Indeed, as the doors shut, I encountered several gasps and expressions of horror from the other elevator passengers. (I can only assume that this is a consequence of becoming more zombie-like, and so regard it is a positive indicator of success.)"*

Over the course of this week, the people with whom you regularly interact will come to expect you to compromise to a lessening degree. Believe me, after a full seven days of the new you, they won't even be asking if you'd mind picking up the kids tonight, if they can talk you into sharing that slice of pie, or if you could focus on "her needs" during lovemaking.

Of course, people who are unaware of your week-long transformation will be in for quite a shock when they see you again.

Remember:

**To compromise or become distracted
is very unlike a zombie.**

**To go unerringly after your goal
is very much like a zombie.**

Nobody tries to negotiate with a zombie.

**As you become more like a zombie, people
will try less and less to negotiate with you.**

Week

3

The Silence of the Zombies

An earlier section has enumerated the many benefits of maintaining a zombie-like silence in most situations. Zombies don't prattle, and zombies don't brag. (What happens in the graveyard **stays** in the graveyard.)

In week 3 of your zombification training, we will see how coupling this zombie silence with the caveats against fear and compromise learned in weeks 1 and 2 can combine to lead you to your next stage as a zombie acolyte.

To review quickly, most zombies do not speak at all. A few zombies can moan or manage a word or two, and fewer still are capable of short sentences. Importantly, even those zombies who can speak do not do so unless it is vitally necessary.

"Necessary to what?" you may ask. What it desires, of course. For a zombie, this is to eat some brains. Let me make this very clear. It is the most important lesson of week 3 training.

Remember:
Whenever a zombie is talking, no matter what
it is talking about, it is only doing so to bring
it closer to its ultimate goal (eating brains).

Most zombie speech is simple and direct, with content that
cannot be mistaken for something it is not (e.g., "braaaaaains
. . . braaaaaaains . . . braaaaaaains . . . "). However, higher
functioning zombies clearly illustrate that it is permissible
for a zombie to use misdirection, impersonation, and even
"small talk" in its verbal interaction **as long as the zombie's ultimate goal (obtaining brains) is served by it.**
Now that the previous weeks' training has inured you to the
un-zombie-like traits of fear and compromise, you can spend
this third week refining and honing your verbal skills to that
of a zombie. It will involve a meticulous paring-down of
your speech until only that which is most vital remains. It
will be difficult, but you will find it most rewarding.

Let's begin by looking closely at a few examples of economic zombie speech. We will see that, in the end, each
instance, however circuitously, serves to bring the zombie
closer to his goal.

Our first example involves a zombie named Karl, a former
chemist at a research facility whose on-the-job exposure to
a certain chemical compounds has had the unforeseen effect

of turning him into a zombie. A few days after his natural passing, the reanimated Zombie-Karl unexpectedly arrives at his job bright and early, seemingly ready for work. As Karl approaches the security post at the entrance, his pale hands clutching his laminated security pass, we can overhear the following exchange:

Security Guard: "Oh hey, good morning Karl. Gee, you're back to work? I heard you were really sick or something . . ."

Zombie Karl: " . . . nope . . . "

After flashing his security pass, the guard dutifully opens the gate, allowing Karl to shuffle inside the facility.

At first, Karl's actions might appear confusing. There was a perfectly delicious security guard standing right there, armed only with a fiberglass baton and certainly not expecting to be bitten in the head. Not only did our zombie seemingly fail to take advantage of the situation, he also went to the added trouble of using speech to avoid the security guard. Yet when we remember our

Zombie Tip: Suck it up!

You never hear zombies complaining about how bad they have it, even when things are at their most unpleasant. The next time you get an extra memo to write at work, the coach tells you two-a-days will start early this year, or a farmer defending his house from a zombie-horde takes out your kneecaps with his shotgun, just suck it up! No complaining allowed for zombies.

cardinal rule, that zombies only use speech towards their brain-noshing end, we maybe begin to make inferences that explain Karl's actions.

Certainly, overpowering the security guard and chowing down would have resulted in Karl's eating **one** brain, but if his goal is to eat **as many brains as possible**, then we begin to see how Karl's counterintuitive zombie behavior makes perfect sense. Once inside his former workplace, Karl will have easy access to several employees and their edible brains. Further, Karl will have the added advantage of surprise, since nobody thinks something dangerous, much less a zombie, could get past the guard outside. So in leaving the security guard's brain regrettably intact, Karl has gained access to an environment where he will be able to feast for hours on an entire laboratory full of easily surprised research scientists.

For our second example, let's meet a zombie named Claudette. Claudette lived in a remote village on the coast of France until an unpleasant fall from a majestic coastal cliff took her life. She was subsequently reanimated as a zombie by a traveling gypsy witch, who was then subsequently eaten by Claudette (you will recall the prior caveats against attempting reanimation). Zombie-Claudette now spends her days lurking along the coast, feeding on the occasional fisherman or British tourist. One of Zombie-Claudette's advantages is her limited (but very effective) use of speech.

See how, in the following representative example, Claudette uses cover of night to approach a pair of early-morning fishermen:

Henri:	"Un moment! Qu'est-ce que c'est ? J'entends quelque chose."
Guy:	"C'est ne pas possible. Nous sommes tout seuls."
Henri:	"Mais je suis **sûr** j'entends quelque chose . . . Peut-être c'est un cheval."
Guy:	" . . . "
Henri:	"Je suis sérieux!"
Guy:	"Un **cheval** . . . ? **Ici** . . . ? Dans **la plage** . . . ? A **quatre heures** du matin?"
Henri:	"Oui."
Zombie-Claudette:	"Niii. Niii."
Henri:	"Voilà. Un cheval."
Guy:	"Bien. Quelle surprise."*

*****Translation**

Henri:	"One second! What was that? I heard something."
Guy:	"That's not possible. We're all alone."
Henri:	"But I'm **sure** I heard something . . . Maybe it was a horse."
Guy:	" . . . "
Henri:	"I'm serious!"
Guy:	"A **horse** . . . ? **Here** . . . ? On **the beach** . . . ? At **four** in the morning?"
Henri:	"Yes."
Zombie-Claudette:	"Neigh. Neigh."
Henri:	"There you go. A horse."
Guy:	"Well, that's a surprise."

Moments later, that lonely cove will echo with cries of "Zut alors!" as Claudette sinks her teeth through the first of two berets in yet another successful use of zombie-speech.

Whereas in our prior example we saw Karl using speech to impersonate his former human incarnation, we see that Zombie-Claudette is able to go a step beyond this by impersonating a French horse. Taken out of context, of course, Claudette's whinnies would appear to have very little to do with eating someone's brain. Yet, in the context of this example, we see that in fact she has everything to gain by horsing it up a bit.

For our final example (in which we will examine yet a third aspect of zombie-speech), let us meet Bucephalus. A mountain man living high in the forgotten crags of West Virginia, he loses his life as part of a long-standing and much celebrated family feud. Bucephalus then finds himself reanimated as a zombie under the authority of a curse involving a violated moonshine still, his illegitimate sister's bloodline, and the wisest and most mystical of all the village hogs.

Upon reanimation, Bucephalus spends his days carrying out a sort of poetic justice by hunting down the men from the opposing family who conspired to kill him and eating their brains. He may be carrying out a folk-tale style of revenge, true, but it is also true that his enemies tend to live close to the burying ground and are the easiest targets for Zombie-Bucephalus.

Like Karl and Claudette, Bucephalus employs speech to
further his purposes. The following example illustrates Bucephalus's particular innovation. Our scenario commences
late one foggy mountain night as Zombie-Bucephalus
knocks loudly on the cabin door of one of his murderers:

Ezekiel:	"Who's there? Who's knockin' on my door in the middle of the night."
Bucephalus:	" . . . Bucephalus."
Ezekiel (wildly):	"Bucephalus??? But it cain't be you. We left you for dead at the bottom of the ravine last Thursday. Who is this really?"
Bucephalus:	"Bucephalus . . ."
Ezekiel:	"Really?"
Bucephalus:	" . . . "
Ezekiel:	"I'm waiting."
Bucephalus:	"Zombie . . . Zombie-Bucephalus . . . "
Ezekiel:	"Ha! I knew it! By the horn of Beelzebub, you done become a zombie!"
Bucephalus:	"Yes . . . "
Ezekiel:	"And what do you want, zombie? To eat my brain? To leave me for dead the same way I left you, I 'spect?"
Bucephalus:	"Just to talk . . . "
Ezekiel (greatly relieved):	"Oh . . . Well in that case, let me get the door."

As one might expect, our vignette will conclude with Eze-
kiel opening the door to his cabin and instantly regretting
it as Bucephalus pounces on him, removes his filthy John
Deere baseball cap, and tucks in.

The important difference between this and our previous examples is that at no time does Bucephalus pretend to be something other than what he is. Karl and Claudette both used speech to give the impression that they were something other than zombies (a living human and a horse, respectively). Bucephalus, on the other hand, was more-or-less forthcoming about his status in the legions of the undead. In his case, speech was used to provide a ruse not about his identity, but about his intentions.

Our example zombies vary, but all of them have a valuable economy to their speech that is worth imitating. They speak no more than is necessary, and only when it brings them closer to their goals.

Your journaling assignment for week 3 is to retroactively analyze your major uses of speech each day at the end of the day. You will go back and recall each important interaction or series of interactions, taking care to note if the speech that you did manage served your purposes or was wasted language. As the week goes by, hope to see a steady decrease in not only the amount of speech that you use, but in the overall importance of it as regards your ultimate goal in any situation.

The speech-interactions you chronicle can be very detailed and extended, or simple one-sentence interactions. In each instance, note what the situation was, your ultimate goal that it served, how close to the economical speech of a zombie you managed to get, and how you would go through this same interaction differently in the future (if at all). Be brutally honest with yourself.

Some examples:

Situation: *Creepy homeless guy at my bus stop won't leave me alone*

Goal: *Get on my bus without getting groped/smeared with excrement*

Speech Used:
"Eww, get away."
"No seriously, leave. Now."
"I don't have any money for you."
"Look, my boyfriend is a lineman, okay?"
"No, not for the Colts, for the fucking phone company, but he could still kick your ass. Come to think of it, so could I."
"Listen buddy, I'm on my way to a job interview, that's why I'm dressed up like this. If you lay one finger on me or get any of that goo coming out of your face on these shoes, I'm going to forget all about it and devote the rest of my day to kicking your ass. Follow me?"

Analysis of Speech Used:

Got the job done, but was a little long-winded for a zombie.

I think I pretty much stayed in zombie form. (Would a zombie have a problem with face-goo?) The escalation right to violence feels right for a zombie. Also, a zombie goes after what it wants, so it made sense to tell the guy that he better not make me change the thing I want from "Putting my best foot forward in the interview" to "Spending a whole goddamn afternoon rolling some homeless guy."

Situation: *Date with Carol from the party the other night*

Goal: *Carol in my bed by midnight, but gone by 2 a.m.*

Speech Used:
"Hey, Carol, nice to see you again. You look really pretty tonight."

"I hear this place is great."

"Fascinating . . . "

"Really? And then what happened?"

"Fascinating . . . "

"Really? And then what happened?"

"Your sister sounds like a special girl."

"Fascinating . . ."

*"It sounds like that overweight girl **deserved** to be kicked out of your sorority."*

*"No way! **I** think Dane Cook is awesome, **too.**"*

"You know, my place is just around the corner."

"Yes, I do have a Dane Cook DVD somewhere we could watch."

"This might be easier in the bedroom, you know."

"Ouch! Too hard!"

"That's better."

"Gee, I wish you could, but my roommate will be getting back soon, and we have a rule about overnight guests. They have to have sex with both of us."

Analysis of Speech Used:

Overall, I think this went pretty well. Got through the whole evening talking just 16 times. Definitely room for some improvement. Should have said "are hot" in place of "look really pretty." Maybe just "Cook" instead of "Dane Cook" next time? Also, could have used "do" in place of "have sex with." Ultimately though, I think my speech stayed true to zombie form because it brought me closer to my original goals.

Keep a journal like this, and you'll take important steps toward honing your speech to a point (and you'll keep things to the point, like a zombie does).

Remember:

Less is always more.

More detailed speech *is* sometimes permitted, but only when absolutely necessary.

To be like a zombie your speech should always take you towards your ultimate goal.

4

Zombies Level All

Even in the middle ages, humans had the sense that certain things were the "great levelers" of life. The lowliest peasant and the highest king still had some things in common. The front-line infantryman shivering in rags and the well-protected knight riding at the back of the army were alike in a few ways (even though they were dissimilar in most). The beautiful princess and the wizened crone shared more than any first glance (or shudder of revulsion) might indicate.

You may have seen the famous medieval woodcut of a mysterious skeletal figure sweeping pieces off of a chessboard. Art historians often erroneously cite this as an illustration of Death configured as the great leveler, claiming both pawns and kings, and leaving no one untouched—the lesson being that all men must die, no matter what their station in life. These academics are *almost* correct.

The true, skeletal leveler is, however, the zombie.

Not to dwell on this mistake (these academic types do seem earnest in their convictions, and they try so hard), but today we know that death is not as unable to be bought as it might first appear. The rich man who can afford the best doctors, to have his blood changed in Brazil, and expensive prostitutes free from venereal disease is likely to stave off the reaper longer than a man without means. The young person from a connected American political dynasty may have the connections to avoid a military draft that claims many a blue-collar kid. The CEO's wife can afford a personal trainer, regular checkups, and fat-free meals flown in from her nutritionist in Zurich. The janitor's wife is lucky to have a supermarket in her neighborhood at all, much less a park safe enough to jog in.

In summary, death may not be able to be bought off completely, but he will clearly agree to go away for a few more years when the price is right. (Note: A few enthusiasts of *The Singularity* have posited that it may be possible to "live long enough to live forever" through a regimen involving the watching of one's diet, taking 250 vitamin pills each day, and writing ponderous, wildly speculative books about the singularity. While these scientists may very well be correct, their path to eternal life seems rather circuitous when compared to the swift reanimation of a zombie.)

Today, on the other hand, it is the zombie who has replaced Death as the incorruptible enforcer of Fate that truly levels all men.

Zombies treat everyone the same, but there are important differences between zombies and the above examples.

Zombies treat everyone the same because everyone **is** the same thing to a zombie. Any combination of ethnic, historic, socio-economic, religious, or other factors go right out

the window when it comes to zombies. Zombies don't discriminate. Zombies don't treat people differently based on how they look, how they dress, or any other factor. It's all the same to a zombie.

Did you ever hear of a zombie who only ate white people, or only ate black people? No way. Zombies are equal opportunity brain-eaters. In cultures that are not diverse, zombies may have stuck to one race or ethnic group simply because they had no other options. But we see repeatedly that when diversity is introduced to a population, zombies don't bat an eyelash. They just sink their teeth right in. Racism, prejudice, and bigotry simply aren't in a zombie's vocabulary.

Zombies don't adopt these magnanimous practices to be "nice" or to foster working or educational environments free from lawsuits and harassment. However, it **does** make them effective. This week, we will work on making sure it makes **you** more effective too.

Whatever you may have been told by teachers, diversity trainers, or your parole officer, bigotry and prejudice is more than just "wrong," "evil," and "not nice." It is also ineffective.

Remember:
A zombie's effectiveness is directly connected to its lack of discrimination.

Your zombification exercises in week 4 will involve training yourself to avoid discrimination of any sort when it comes to people. No matter what the situation, zombies stick to this policy, even when direct appeals to discrimination are made. Consider the following illustrative examples:

Example One

Between battles, Josiah Young, Master-Sergeant in the 43rd Illinois Artillery, accidentally stumbles into a slave graveyard on a liberated southern plantation where mysterious ancient rites have caused a recently deceased enslaved African-American named Dave to walk the earth again.

Josiah:	"Lands! But that grave yonder is opening! Methinks the dead walk again!"
Dave:	"Brains . . ."
Josiah:	"Steady now, friend. I mean you no harm, but do not approach farther!"
Dave:	"Brains . . ."
Josiah:	"Curses, my revolver does nothing against this foe. And he draws ever nearer!"
Dave:	"Brains . . ."
Josiah:	"Ahh, but in the moonlight I see now that you are . . . or were . . . one of the unjustly enslaved negroes that the Grand Army of the Republic has fought so bravely to set free. Come, my African friend, we must embrace in brotherhood and build a new nation, one in which a man is not judged by his skin's color, but rather by the—"
Dave:	"Brains . . ."
Josiah:	"As you say . . . His brains. Now, if you wouldn't mind unhanding me . . . Um, friend . . ."

Exegesis: Here we have a wonderful example of a zombie leveling the self-righteous man and bringing him down to where the rest of us are. It just goes to show that good works are no security against zombies. Our Yankee friend earnestly believed that the blood he and his comrades had shed at Shiloh and Bull Run would somehow "count" in his favor. Not when the zombies come knocking. For his part, our zombie, Dave, is at no point distracted by his victim's tales of self-sacrifice and earnest vision for a peaceful future where Americans live together in tolerance and prosperity. He's not going to think about one victim being more or less worthy than another. Whether it's a bigoted slavemaster or an idealistic Union soldier, Dave is chowing down. Truly, all men are equal in his eyes, and in his mouth.

Example Two

On Prom Night 2007 in Davenport, Iowa, Davenport North football star Jason Panther wanders away from the after-prom party on the banks of the Mississippi. Suddenly, walking up the riverbank he sees the skulking form of Carol Snogley, the yearbook editor and president of the Chess Club, who threw herself into the river after a prank by the football team (and several cheerleaders) involving some Photoshopped images of Carol and the assistant principal, and resulting in an emergency PTA meeting and a segment on *20/20*. A recent government chemical spill into the river (also covered on *20/20*) has had an unforeseen effect on Carol.

Jason:	"Carol? Carol Snogley? Is that *you*?"
Carol:	"Jason . . . "
Jason:	"Omigod. Carol, we are all **so sorry** about what happened. Nobody expected those pictures to get so much attention. You wouldn't believe the fallout. I got suspended for every away game that's not

	part of the IHSAA tournament. Some of the cheerleaders got it even worse. I'm not even kidding."
Carol:	"Jason . . ."
Jason:	"Gee, is that the same dress you were wearing when you jumped off the bridge? We all thought you were dead. It was on *20/20* and everything. We should let everybody know you're okay. I'd go tell people myself, but the way you're shuffling over to me makes my legs feel sort of frozen. It's the darndest thing."
Carol:	"Brains . . ."
Jason:	"Gee, can't move at all. Funny how that happens."
Carol:	"Brains . . ."
Jason:	"You know, Carol, I never told you how I secretly thought you were really cool. I mean, I know I used to laugh or make a 'thpppt' noise every time you got an answer right in class, but really, I thought it was . . . neat. And when the cheerleaders would tease you about your clothes being from a Mexican outlet store, I knew that wasn't true. Looking back, yes, I should have said something."
Carol:	"Brains . . ."
Jason:	"I never told **anybody** this, but I always felt like **I** was more of a nerd than a jock. I mean, my dad's always pushing me to play sports. And whatever, maybe I set the Iowa State High School Football record for most forced fumbles in a season this year, but that's not who I am. I like . . . books, and reading and things. I

even saw *Star Wars*. It was the new ones, but, and this is being one hundred percent honest, I thought that Jar Jar Binks guy was dope."

Carol: "Brains . . ."

Jason: "I guess what I'm trying to say, it being prom night and all, is . . . There's a whole group of kids who were also in on the prank just five minutes walk from here. They're passed out in sleeping bags and it would be **way** easier for you to eat them. Let me go and I can show you right where they are. How 'bout it Carol? One nerd to another . . . Carol . . . ? Carol . . . ?"

Exegesis: In this example, Jason tries to save his skin from a zombie-nerd by claiming to secretly be a nerd himself. Later, he essays to prolong his life by insinuating that he can be useful to a zombie, if given the chance. Carol's obvious declension shows how zombies refuse to give special treatment. Jason's tale about identifying as a nerd was a lie (except for the Jar Jar Binks part), but whether or not he was lying made no difference to Carol. Jock or nerd, his brain was still her dinner. No preferential treatment. As for the offer of other victims, well, let's just say it doesn't take a nerd (or a zombie nerd) to know that hungover kids

---

Zombie Tip:
A brain a day (is still not enough brains).

And don't worry about keeping the doctor away. If he sees you, he's going to run off on his own.

aren't going anywhere for quite a while. (They might make a fine banquet, but it's open all night, and there's no reason why Jason shouldn't be the appetizer.)

Example Three

Paris Raddison, hotel heiress and famous nudist, visits a new luxury spa in the American Southwest for treatment of "nervous exhaustion," with no idea that the spa's developers ignored the protestations of a local Native American tribe that reminded them the land had been a hallowed burial ground since time immemorial. As Paris relaxes in a seaweed-chipotle body wrap and mud bath, a zombie named Two-Crow climbs in through the window and chows down on the aromatherapy expert before Paris can tell her which scented candles she'd like for the lavender and beeswax massage.

Paris:	"Hey, that is so not hot."
Two-Crow:	"Brains . . ."
Paris:	" Do you even **know** who my father is?"
Two-Crow:	"Brains . . ."
Paris:	"What does that even mean? Are you saying I'm not smart, like in those stupid tabloids? I'll have you know that I got into Choate. I even wrote a book about how to be fabulous and stuff, with a lady who followed me around and wrote down the things I said and how awesome they were. Hear that? I WROTE A BOOK. That means I'm smart. Don't tell me I don't have brains."

Two-Crow:	"Eat . . . Brains . . . "
Paris:	"Oh what? You want to eat my brain, just like you ate the brain of that stupid aromatherapy lady? You don't 'get' to eat my brain like that, mister. She was Mexican and probably poor. Her family was probably poor. Maybe even illegal immigrants. **I'm** Paris Raddison. My life is good. My brain doesn't get eaten. Got it?"
Two-Crow:	"Brains . . . "
Paris (slightly less sure of herself):	"Got it . . . ?"

Exegesis: We've already reviewed how zombies are impervious to flattery and temptation. This example shows how they are also immune to distinctions of social class, even when directly invoked. Ms. Raddison's feelings of entitlement (based on wealth, race, status, fame, and the publication of a ghostwritten book) did not register with our zombie. Likewise, the attempt made by Paris to show the zombie substantive ways in which she was "different" from the hapless aromatherapist failed utterly.

Two-Crow "treated" both young women the same, and because of this, he was successful in his project.

During this week, you will work to ensure that your day-to-day interactions with others mirror the equanimity shown by zombies in the above examples.

In your journal, make a list of significant interactions in which you followed the example of a zombie and did not take into account the external differences of the people with whom you dealt. These interactions can involve dialogue, but it is not a requirement. They can involve actions taken, or, importantly, actions NOT taken, because of someone's attributes.

Be sure to record the scenario, the appeal made to you based on an external quality, your zombie-like response, and your evaluation of it.

Example One

Scenario: Sally, the receptionist at my job, asks me if I want to buy a candy bar for five dollars (five dollars!) to help her daughter's school afford a class trip to Washington, D.C.

Appeal: Judging by Sally's pay-grade, zip code, and single mom status, this candy bar thing is probably the only way her daughter's going to be able to afford to go. The appeal is economic.

Response: I didn't buy a candy bar because of Sally's strong insinuation that her daughter needed the money for the trip. I **did,** however, buy three of them because it still beats walking to the basement of Building C to hit the vending machines whenever I need a snack.

Evaluation: Outwardly, it might look like I failed this test and let myself feel sorry for a co-worker's child. I know, however, that I would have bought these candy bars from the CEO himself. (Observation: He wouldn't need the money like Sally, but buying candy cars from the CEO might look as though I was attempting to curry favor. Perhaps there is no way to avoid this problem . . .)

Example Two

Scenario: My wife and I are sitting in the entrance to the diner on Sunday, waiting to be seated for brunch. This old couple from our congregation comes in and starts insinuating that they'd really like us to give up our seats. ("What a long service today, huh?" "My wife has a bad hip, you know," "I just don't have the energy I used to," etc.)

Appeal: I'm supposed to "feel sorry" for them because they're old, right?

Response: Before I can even do anything (like say "No way, you old fogies"), my wife stands up and offers the woman her seat. I don't move at first, but when the old biddy sits down, she starts right in with the nattering ("I remember when this place first opened." "Do you know our grandson Nate who sings in the choir?" "Did you hear about the pastor's youngest brother? He went to San Francisco and married another man.") After a few minutes, I didn't want to sit there anymore, so I let her husband take the seat."

Evaluation: Overall good, but maybe some room for improvement. I wouldn't have given up my seat to the old couple, even though they were old, except after a while I started to want to. I didn't let them "appeal" to me with their oldness, and I didn't treat them differently than I'd treat anybody else. Eventually I wanted to move, but I'd want to move if any annoying person sat next to me, so really it's my wife's fault for letting this happen. (Possible next step: convince wife to consider *Zen of Zombie* 90-Day zombification program for herself?)

Example Three

Scenario: Matt, the dreamy assistant professor for my Intro to Economics class, hints that we could "discuss" my D+ this weekend over some wine in his apartment. I've had a crush on him since the first day of class, but I've heard that it's bad for students to hook up with their professors. I forget how it goes exactly . . . Something about getting myself expelled and ruining a man's career.

Appeal: Maybe his status? Oh, and his ability to change my grade. But really, what "appeals" to be is his hot little butt and that tasteful pony tail.

Response: Totally rocked his world for most of Friday night and some of Saturday morning. Kind of a letdown, though . . . He looks a lot better up at the lectern than he does in a

69. And afterward he got all weird and kept saying: "You can't tell anybody about this. This is my last chance at a tenure-track job. It's just that there's nobody to date at a rural college like this."

Evaluation: I didn't treat Matt differently than any other campus hottie I wanted to take to bed, so I think it's totally fine. Also, just like any other guy I take to bed, I'm totally going to blog about our time together on my MySpace, and it's the rules that he HAS to give me a big hug when we see each other around campus. (Question: Does that include in the class he teaches? I say yes.)

Now and then, a Nazi skinhead zombie stumbles into a Jewish neighborhood and starts eating some serious Ashkenazi brain. And it's easy for onlookers to guess that the zombie has carried his bigotry with him into the afterlife. Once a bigot, always a bigot, they'll say. Even in death, this insecure thug needs a group to feel better than. The truth of the matter may be more banal. Usually, it is random chance that leads a Nazi zombie to the Jewish part of town. Or a Jewish zombie to a Palestinian part of town. Or a Serb zombie to Little Croatia, and so on.

You've probably experienced this in your own life, prior to reading this book. How many times have you come to dislike someone of another race or religion (not **because of** their race or religion, but because they were a jerk), and yet hesitated to let it be known for fear of being branded a racist? In particular cases, zombies might appear to be favoring one type of person over another, but it's just a coincidence. One has to trust that a zombie would never act in a bigoted or prejudiced way.

When you come right down to it, you always lose when you treat people differently based on how they look or what they make. You create hate in the world, sure, but you also make yourself less effective, less adaptable, and you decrease your own chances for getting what you want in life.

It's great that governments, corporations, and schools are catching on to the fact that diversity is a strength. But credit where credit is due. It's a rule that zombies have been playing by since the beginning of time.

Remember:

A zombie treats everybody the same, regardless of race, religion, income, or other factors.

A zombie also doesn't worry about appearing prejudiced when its actions coincidentally line up with historical prejudices (e.g., an Indian zombie eating a Pakistani victim, or vice versa).

Above all, a zombie understands that diversity is a strength.

5

Pax Zombana

World leaders are frequently (and rightly) lauded when they take steps to make a lasting impact for peace throughout the world. Truly, there can be no greater calling. Those who strive to rid the earth of war, senseless violence, and criminal atrocities deserve our highest accolades. Gandhi, King, Mandela, Carter, Bono . . . The list goes on and on. Yet the most famous award for this work, the Nobel Peace Prize, has never once been bestowed upon one beyond the realm of the living.

While it would be difficult to locate one zombie, out of all possible "living" zombies, who is most deserving of the Nobel, its recent presentation to groups like Doctors Without Borders and the Grameen Bank (as opposed to an individual person) encourages those who would like to see Zombies as a group named the winner. Not everyone likes the idea of the King of Sweden presenting his country's highest accolade to a reanimated corpse in tails, but few can dispute the positive international effect of zombies.

When it comes to encouraging peace and harmony, there are two ways in which zombies deserve recognition. The first is by serving as a living example of peace. (It is this idea that will constitute the lesson for this chapter.)

The second way zombies create peace is to encourage allegiances between nations and persons. Though secondary to this chapter's zombification lesson, it remains important to point out that zombies, by their very presence in any substantial number, have contributed to the disappearance of prejudices and the formation of new peaceful alliances . . . namely, alliances against zombies. Throughout history, many a warring nation-state, when faced with a rampaging zombie horde, has called for a cease fire, and literally combined forces with its historical enemies to present a united force against the undead. Are zombies credited with inspiring this cooperation and good feeling (which can last years after the zombies are defeated)? Almost never, and never adequately.

On a micro-level, zombies have long helped small groups of people put aside personal squabbles, forge lasting bonds (sometimes even romantic ones worthy of an R-rating), and usher in a cooperative zeal. For example, family reunions are often filled with bickering, malice, and silent loathing. Have a detachment of zombies attack that same family reunion, and you're going to see teamwork, bonding, and the casting aside of old grudges as the family combines forces to protect their small rural farmhouse from the hungry invaders. Zombies have a way of putting things into perspective for people. A drunk brother-in-law or a spinster aunt's constantly needling can appear substantially less oppressive when brain-eating corpses begin to lay siege.

On a macro-level, we see zombies helping to build community and forge alliances between all types of people. Nations that have been at war for generations often find their citizens suckling at the teat of the myth of historical oppression. "Why do things suck so much? Because of Country X, our historical oppressors!" (When in truth, life usually just sucks all the time, and for no reason.) This myth that the suckiness of life is somebody (or some country's fault) will inspire generation after generation into combat. The spell of the myth can only be lifted when a real, honest threat, that actually has the potential to make your life suck—like by eating you—shambles onto the battlefield. Throughout time, historical enemies have set aside their differences to build coalitions against a common enemy. And brother, there's no enemy more common than zombies.

So whether it's coalition-building between empires or a rural scuffle that makes one family remember how much it has in common after all, zombies inspire humans to unity and solidarity better than almost anything.

Our present concern, however, is the positive way in which zombies comport themselves within the community of zombies. Namely, in perfect peace.

Ask yourself, of the many discouraging crime statistics paraded by the media, did you ever hear of a problem of "zombie-on-zombie" violence?

Did you ever hear of any zombie-on-zombie violence at all, ever?

The reason you didn't is that zombies are the most peaceful and cohesive group in the world, living or dead. Human groups bicker and fight internally almost as much as they do with their enemies. Certain ethnic groups historically haven't gotten along, and this has been reflected in clashes between their communities, but these same groups **also** exhibit infighting, crime, and struggle within their own barrios, 'hoods, and trailer parks. Zombies fight (for the flesh of the living) and scrap as much as any other ethnic group (probably a lot more), but back at the graveyard, their inter-community relations can only be described as idyllic.

Here some would posit that a contrast of the living with the living dead may be unfair and flawed. However, a quick survey will reveal that the zombie's supernatural brethren are not exempt from the infighting common to humans.

Vampires, for example, are extremely jealous of one another. The leadership of their various sects or gangs is constantly contested. They engage in machinations of political intrigue as in a medieval court, with each vampire struggling to curry favor and advance his or her place in the line for the throne. Many estimate that exponentially more vampires are staked by jealous colleagues than are ever impaled by intrepid vampire-hunters or enterprising priests.

Werewolves, operating in "packs" as they do, have similar leadership issues. The need to assert oneself as a "dominant male" is frequently a werewolf's undoing.

Mummies, because of their isolation, are largely untested in this area. Based upon a mummy's tendency to return to its sarcophagus when unwanted visitors are eliminated, many suspect that mummies would more or less exist peacefully if they ever were to encounter another of their kind. (As has been previously noted, mummies are probably the most similar to zombies of any netherworld creature. Hence their many positive qualities.)

Unlike most of their supernatural compatriots, zombies exist in a brotherhood of peace. This instinctual comraderie eliminates the need for a "leader," or any sort of hierarchy at all. Zombies can take or leave the respect of their peers, and when your only real goal is eating brains, the advantages of elected or appointed office are minimal.

Of course, research into the world of the "zombie at rest" is not as plentiful as into that of the "zombie on the rampage." Nonetheless, there is evidence enough to suggest that when zombies are not "on" (that is, there are no humans around to eat), they exist in a world of quiet, dignified fellowship. There is no argument or hate speech in this world, or speech at all. There is nothing like a police force in the world of zombies, because there is no crime to necessitate it.

Many different positive qualities combine in zombies to

form this ideal society of peace, but perhaps no one more so than this:

Zombies do not hold grudges.

You know the phrase "Like water off a duck's back?" It should be more like "Like a grudge off a zombie's desiccated flesh." No one shrugs things off like the zombified.

Don't think for a moment that zombies live in some ideal fantasy world, either. They live in the same world as you or me, full of disappointments, dashed hopes, and king-sized letdowns. There's been no research into whether zombies feel disappointment now and then—but if they do, they don't show it.

A zombie's world revolves around brains.

So, really, the only thing one zombie might do to offend another is to eat a human's brain first, before any other zombies can. When your whole day revolves around trying to find and eat brains, you'd think this would be a crushing letdown for a zombie. Imagine it. You've had this fleeing human in your sights for hours, chasing it all around an abandoned mall. Then, just when you've got it cornered, one of your zombie buddies jumps in out of nowhere and beats you to the prize.

The thing is, this scenario happens **all the time** in the world of zombies, and yet no zombie-on-zombie resentment ever foments. Zombies frequently work in groups to break down storm doors, crash through plate glass, and corral humans into abandoned buildings. Most of the time, only a few of the zombies involved actually get to enjoy the spoils of the horde's efforts. Many times, the zombies who do the most work (breaking windows, dodging vehicles, getting shot at) have the least success when its time to actually eat a brain or two.

Yet remarkably, no zombie is deterred by this prospect, even as it occurs time and time again.

And apparently, no zombie feels jealousy toward the ones who do feed. The zombie in the front of the pack never wavers in his pursuit of the government troops, even though their impressive arsenal makes it painfully clear than many waves of zombies will be eliminated before any of them even gets a chance to eat a brain.

Zombie Tip:
Many hands make light work.

However, these same hands can be magically delicious for a zombie. There's no reason work and snack time can't mete out some kind of compromise though, you know?

The zombie whose colleague has eaten ten brains that day, and he none, shows no disdain for his talented friend, and is no less plucky in the continual pursuit of his first one. Zombies infer nothing from how their own success or failure compares to that of their colleagues. It's not a race with zombies (except when they're racing after a human). Your winning doesn't make me a loser, and so on. There are an almost infinite number of humans, so it's basically a non-zero sum game.

Compared to zombies, humans seem to be obsessed with their success or failure when compared to that of their peers. Humans watch one another. The smallest uptick in fortune is noted, and the smallest failure is likewise privately recorded. These changes and their impact prompt humans to envy, revenge, violence, and all manner of crimes. Where zombies could give a fuck about how they compare to the guy standing next to them, humans are obsessed with it to a point of detriment, to the point where it hampers their effectiveness and hurts their ability to get on with their lives.

But you don't have to be.

As our exercise for week 5, you will construct a list of all persons in your life for whom you harbor any negative feelings related to their success or failure. This should not include persons you simply dislike for their character or for some other reason (bad breath, clinginess, attempted murder). We all have sworn enemies upon whom we would wish no success ever, but this is not a list for those people. This list is for people whom we resent **because of** their success.

Along with the person's name, give a little descripton of who they are and their relation to you, the precise nature of the grudge, and how you currently express your feelings when you're around this person.

When finished, it should look similar to this:

Name: Charlie Johnson

Description: College roommate

Grudge: Spent his whole college experience, including two senior years, drinking my beer and playing Quake while I took honors classes and worked two jobs. Ten years later, I'm little more than a secretary with a fancy title, and Charlie runs his father's yarn factory in Ohio for six figures a year (and has a four-hour workday).

Current tactic: I just try to avoid Charlie altogether. Now and then he'll come through town on "business" but I usually make up an excuse not to see him. At our last college reunion, I got drunk enough that he would think my attitude was just the booze talking. It wasn't.

Name: Dustin Moore

Description: Friend from work

Grudge: Dustin is my age, but acts like he's about 15. He dresses badly, has never worked out a day in his life, and is always broke. He's inarticulate, regularly makes off-color jokes, and believed the *Blair Witch Project* was real for like five years or something. Despite this, women everywhere love him. Whether at the office or out at a bar, he's got ladies all over him. It makes no sense, but there it is. In contrast, I'm responsible, smart, and keep myself in way better shape than Dustin. Despite this, I've been on only three dates in the past five years, and two of those were with women I met through Dustin. **What the hell!?**

Current tactic: Small but numerous passive-aggressive actions throughout the day. I sabotage his projects, "forget" to include him in important meetings, and have subscriptions to pornographic magazines sent to him at the office (the girls in the mail room just think it's "cute"). I also make a point to keep new female employees away from him, but they always come over to say hi eventually. I'm thinking of circulating a VD rumor about him next quarter, but part of me knows it's not even going to make a dent.

Name: Tad Smith

Description: My slackass older brother

Grudge: So, Tad, who never finished a thing in his life, including three different tries at college, calls me up like a year ago and says he has this idea for writing a movie screenplay where this retired cop gets a heart transplant, but what no one knows is that it was the heart of a psycho-killer the police have been looking for. So then the heart possesses him and HE goes out and starts being a psycho-killer, but the police are still following their leads for the OLD psycho-killer. When the police finally do get on his trail, he gets shot and, wait for it, he has to have ANOTHER heart transplant. But check it, they put the killer's heart in a THIRD person, so then the hero has to help the police catch this other person before HE starts being the psycho-killer.

I told Tad to forget about it and instead concentrate on getting an associate's degree or a job or something.

Anyhow, last month it got optioned by Twentieth-Century Fox for $100,000 plus points, and Jack Nicholson is attached. I hate my life.

Current tactic: Crying in my beer. Wincing whenever family members talk about how "successful" Tad is. Also, I've been trying to get up the nerve to ask him if I can visit the set and meet Nicholson. (Really like *The Shining*.)

You may have more (or possibly fewer) subjects on your list. It doesn't matter. The important thing for our purposes is your ability to identify the nature of your grudge, and that you be honest about how you're currently dealing with it (or not dealing with it, as the case may be).

Once you have your list finished, we'll need to take a leap of faith via a thought experiment that may seem fanciful at first (but bear with me). Pretend, for a moment, that the offenses committed by those who have wronged you, were not done unto you, but instead, to a zombie. Unlikely, yes, but give it a shot.

Next, ask yourself how a zombie would react to this situation. A zombie wouldn't hold a grudge, but what **would** it do? You can be as specific or as general as you like. If your first idea about a zombie's reaction doesn't feel right, then give it some time and come back to it after a break. Think about everything we've learned about zombies up to this point. When you think you have an idea, go ahead and make a new list of how a zombie would react in each instance. For example:

Situation: My slacker roommate from college is now set for life with a sinecure he doesn't begin to deserve.
Zombie reaction: I don't think a zombie would care. A zombie might eat him, but only if he were, you know, around.

Situation: Guy at work inexplicably gets more tail than Ron Jeremy.
Zombie reaction: Nothing. Zombies aren't into the ladies. Or men. Or sex at all.

Situation: Undeserving brother sells a screenplay out of nowhere.

Zombie reaction: I guess nothing. Maybe visit the set to eat people.

Noticing a pattern? The goal here is not to make you feel foolish, but to drive home the way that a zombie lets everything roll off. A zombie's inability to hold a grudge is not just an abstract idea. It can apply to the grudges in your life, too.

For the final step of this exercise, go once more over your examples and compare and contrast your way of coping with (or reacting to) these people against a zombie's way. Take your time, and note the benefits of each. Specifically, I'd like you to note what your reaction "costs" you in terms of energy and effort (contrasted with that of a zombie), and what your reaction has the potential to accomplish (contrasted with that of a zombie).

The finished product could look something like this:

Situation: College roommate gets more than he deserves.

My response: Avoidance, public intoxication.

Zombie response: More or less nothing.

Evaluation: My response leads to pretty much nothing, except for looking like I turned out a drunk in front of my old professors. Involves lying and ingesting nine gin and tonics.

Zombie response also accomplishes nothing.

Situation: Guy at work gets all the tail.

My response: Sabotage, prankery, misdirection of female employees.
Zombie response: More or less nothing.

Evaluation: My way involves coming up with brilliant pranks, but does cost me some lost work hours. My pranks don't work though, which just makes me hate him more. The zombie way is just doing nothing, but I guess it wouldn't make me madder every day.

Situation: Undeserving brother gets glamorous payday.

My response: Sullenness. Secret desire to meet famous actors.
Zombie response: More or less nothing.

Evaluation: My way does nothing, except makes me feel depressed. The cost is I'm bummed. Maybe if I'm nice to him and look pitiful, I get to visit the set. The zombie way also does nothing. A zombie probably isn't depressed, though. And, again, he could still go to the set to eat famous people if he wanted a change of pace.

What I hope these (and your) results illustrate, is that the best outcome in most of these cases is nothing. The best possible reaction is no reaction at all.

The zombie way is also cheaper. Deciding instantly that you will not resent someone costs nothing. In the other above examples, we see costs. We see over-consumption of alcohol, man-hours lost on the job, and somebody looking all sullen in front of Jack Nicholson. None of these costs "does" anything to settle the score with the person we envy. The person holding the grudge, on the other hand, stands to hurt himself in each different instance.

When you let someone make you hold a grudge, you give them power over you.

Remember:

That a zombie does not hold a grudge is directly to the zombie's advantage.

It's not the case that zombies are so powerful that grudges don't concern them. Rather, they choose not to hold grudges, and this makes them powerful.

Week

6

What's That Rule?
Play It Cool.

Wherever they are, whomever they're with, and whatever the situation, zombies have a way of making the best of things.

No, wait, that's actually selling it short a bit.

Zombies don't just make the best of things. At least not in the way regular people do.

When they get knocked down, they spring right back to life.

When their situation looks bad, they don't pause for an instant—**not for one instant**—to be depressed about it, before continuing on their way.

When forces that promise almost certain doom to a zombie array themselves before it, a zombie doesn't flinch (though some higher-functioning zombies **have** been known to smile).

A zombie doesn't just "make the best of it." Rather, a zombie is like a resilience-machine, designed to stay on course no matter what. Words like *ennui, hesitation, doubt,* and *depression* aren't even in its vocabulary.

There is every indication that, at every moment it exists, a zombie is doing what it loves, and loving what it does. The quest for brains is not something that a zombie's going to let come second for any reason. Keenly aware that becoming flustered, or depressed, or in any way emotionally distracted does not further its purposes, a zombie simply chooses not to lose its cool.

Have you ever heard anybody talk about a zombie that had lost its cool? You'll also never hear someone talk about a zombie "flying off the handle and trying to eat someone's brain." This is because zombies are already after your brain, which is as "off the handle" as it gets, really.

Have you ever heard of an angry zombie? (True, zombies can *appear* angry when compared to humans, but think in terms of "compared to other zombies.")

How about a sad zombie? (A zombie standing by itself out in the rain might seem, for a second, like a pitiful sight. But trust me, that thing is feeling no pain. Zombies aren't humans, as should be painfully clear by this point.)

A zombie doesn't wince at what most of us would call a "des-

perately dire situation" and "a tragically grave misfortune."
The average human is not so lucky.

Remember:

Zombies don't let emotions bring them down.
Or up. Zombies stay in control.

It doesn't take much to bum out your typical person. A parking ticket can do it. An unexpected visit from an in-law, likewise. A lousy horoscope reading? Sure, for some people.

The impact of our misfortunes is usually far less than we give them credit for. The lasting negative impacts of these events are usually nothing. They are temporary inconveniences, or minor pains that will be over soon. Yet humans have a way of "catastrophizing" and concentrating upon the worst possible implications of a situation or circumstance.

A bad performance review at work, and we suddenly decide we're about to be fired, and will never get another job, and are literally just weeks from living on a friend's couch.

A rash on our shoulder that won't go away, and we're convinced it's melanoma and we can count on being dead by this time next year.

A policeman at the door to ask if we've seen a missing neighbor kid, and our mind goes right to the mail-fraud ring we've been running out of the basement, and before we know what we're saying we're on our knees confessing it all to the man in blue and begging him to put in a word for leniency with the judge.

In summary, we really suck at keeping our cool compared to zombies. At the first sign of a potentially adverse circumstance, we're apt to crumble like a crumb cake.

Zombies, on the other hand, excel at playing it cool.

They are masters of making the best of a situation and keeping their composure. And you can be too, if you're willing to make like a zombie.

The importance of this week's lesson cannot be overemphasized. To drive home the point, for this week's zombification exercises you're going to make a Greatest Hits of Losing My Cool list.

Think back over the last five-to-ten years of your life and try to picture the times that you really lost your cool. Times when lack of emotion would have been to your advantage, but when your emotions won anyway. Remember the situation you were in when it happened. Remember how emotion made you act, and what losing your cool made you do. If there was a specific act or phrase that crystallized the moment when coolness was lost, jot it down. Then, finally and most importantly, write down what losing your cool cost you. (If you need to speculate a little here, that's fine.)

You may have many instances of losing your cool, or you may have just a few. If you're a reserved person, it may be a stretch to think of something, and that's okay. Remember, it doesn't have to be dramatic and obvious, like hazarding your life savings at the roulette table. It simply needs to be a situation where you remember having a less-than-optimal outcome because of your emotions.

Your finished list should look something like this:

Example One

Situation: So Werner Herzog was on this panel at UCLA and I really wanted to go because I am such a fan. It's supposed to be for students only, but I had my old ID and I thought I could get it to work. We get up to the box office though, and the guy is all like, "This says you graduated in 2005. You realize this is the line for student tickets, don't you? *Sir?*"

Loss of cool: So the guy was a bit of a snark, and I knew I should've just let it go, but when he called me sir, I was like, I'm just 25! And he's all, get in the regular line with everybody else or I'm calling security. And I could have totally taken the guy, but I was worried about security coming because there was a ton of shit I did back in 2005 that they never caught me on, so I just chickened out, really.

Embodiment of loss of cool: "Whatever. I'm going to the other line, just because you suck." But it wasn't because he sucked, it was because I'd let him make me afraid.

Consequences/Cost: No Werner Herzog.

Example Two

Situation: The big spring dance, senior year of college. Went with Jane Lundermann, not really the most attractive girl, or the smartest, but she kind of had a reputation as a girl who would go all the way on a first date. I'm thinking whatever . . . It's senior year, and I'm not looking to fall in love. My dad's already told me that he'll pay for me to backpack around Europe for a year after graduation, and then I am so going to art school for an MFA. Maybe Rhode Island, maybe Art Institute. All I know for sure is that I want to spend the next fifty years making plaster casts of animal genitalia.

Loss of cool: So after the dance winds down, a bunch of us end up behind the science building doing coke and before I know it I'm so revved up I can't see straight. Jane is too. We go back to her dorm room and start to get it on.

Embodiment of loss of cool: "Omigod Jane, that's **so** much better without the stupid condom."

Consequences/Cost: Missed period. Shotgun wedding after graduation. No Europe trip or MFA. And I'm working nine to fucking five (instead of making molds of animal bits) to support a stupid wife and kid.

Example Three

Situation: We're driving back from the Fox Head one night and get pulled over. Not anything out of the ordinary, except that just as the cop gets out of his car, Sammy turns to us in the back seat and goes, "Dudes, just so you know, that backpack at your feet is totally full of weed."

Loss of cool: So while the one cop is breathalizing Sammy (he so totally failed it), another one gets out and stalks around

---

Zombie Tip:

If a brain is produced in the first act, it must be eaten in the last.

Everything happens for a reason. Yeah, I'm talking to you, Mr. Cynical Atheist Curmudgeon Guy. When the universe throws something tempting your way—like, hmm, I don't know, a tantalizing brain—you may not get it right away. But just be patient. It's there for a reason. Guns have a way of being shot. Brains have a way of getting eaten. At least eventually.

the side and shines his flashlight in on us. I don't even think he shined his light on the backpack intentionally, but the moment the beam even gets near it, Rajat starts screaming "That's backpack's not mine! It's not mine. It's totally this guy's." And he points over at Sammy, but because of where he's standing it looks just like he's pointing right at me."

Embodiment of loss of cool: I don't remember exactly, but I was getting frisked at one point and I remember, clearly, coming out with something like: "Take your hands off me, you redneck goon. My taxes pay your salary."

Consequences/Cost: Thirty months, under the stupid new minimum-sentencing laws.

Let's be clear: Zombies have been called "extreme" in the same way that snowboarding is an "extreme sport." Usually, the adjective is invoked this way by enthusiasts. While zombies may be "extreme" in this sense, they do not operate in extremes moment to moment.

When your whole existence is spent walking the earth in search of living human brains to consume, your very way of being in the world is an extremity. However, zombies pursue this extreme goal with a reservation and aplomb that is nothing if not conservative and dignified.

When zombies break down a farmhouse door, it is only because that door has buckled under the gentlemanly pressure of **many** zombies, who have pushed hard, but **not** extremely hard. (You don't see zombies flexing and emoting like professional wrestlers or weightlifters. Their exertion is more dignified than that.)

When a zombie chases a victim into a corner, it is not at a sprinter's wild and hoary gallop, but with an easy and confident saunter.

Whatever the situation, zombies play it cool.

For the rest of week 6, you should make a concerted effort to play it cool in every situation.

In every task, ask yourself not only

"Is this what a zombie would do?"

but also

"Is this how a zombie would do it?"

Love Zombie

Everyone wants to find love in life.

Platonic love. Fraternal love. Rutting-like-an-animal love, sure. But **especially** romantic love. A self-help book, even one about zombies, would not be worth its salt if it didn't include a guide to maximizing your romantic potential. After all, you deserve love. You have the right to love and feel loved. And you're probably sick of sitting and waiting around for that love to appear.

"But wait," I hear you saying, "aren't zombies sexless beings, utterly incapable of showing love? Don't they lack entirely the inclination to physical romance or emotional openness? Wasn't there a previous section of this book ("Bros before hos") about how zombies show no interest at all in the opposite sex (or the same sex)?

It is true that zombies don't show love (or feel love), but it turns out that their tactics prove expert for obtaining it. Remember, zombies go after what they want. Zombies want brains, but you might want a loving mate with whom you can raise a family and grown old. Don't worry. This impulse is not contrary to your zombification. Rather, because virtually all humans have desires to this end, it is very like a zombie to go out and get the man or woman (or even the she-male from the back page of the *Village Voice*) of your dreams.

In this week's lesson, we will learn how the tactics of a zombie prove expert in the quest for love, and we'll put those tactics into action.

We've talked before about how zombies are good at shattering misconceptions and stereotypes. Love is full of misconceptions.

- *Men only want sex.*
- *Women only want attention and prescience and expensive presents.*

There are others, sure. Too many to list here. But the biggest misconception shattered by zombies is that the chase is better than the catch.

Even though this position has been long maintained by many (verbatim, in fact, by no less a netherworld expert than Lemmy Kilmister), it is one readily shattered by the zombie.

For reasons unknown, the stereotype persists that, once obtained, love is never as good as we think it will be. Or that love necessarily fades over time. Sadly, this falsehood keeps some people from going after love at all. It is true that bad relationships (and, of course, bad sex) do sometimes happen, and that courtship, will all its razzle-dazzle and bank account-clearing expenditure, can seem more compelling than the prize at which it is all directed.

Yet true love remains a real and compelling possibility for many, and a bad past relationship is no reason to write off dating as an exercise in disappointment.

Zombies know all about the chase.
And the catch.

And no matter what your cynical sewing circle or drunken frat buddies have told you, the chase is nothing compared to the catch.

While romantic humans involved in "the chase" face humiliating rejection, painstaking preparation processes, and the prospect of blowing a whole goddamn paycheck for a kiss on the cheek on a Friday night, zombies have it even worse. A zombie on "the chase" faces everything from fortifications hastily constructed in an abandoned house, to full-fledged military arsenals directed against him. A chasing zombie (which is most zombies, most of the time) faces bullets, explosives, and voodoo spells, but that's not stopping it. Because a zombie wants what it wants. And the zombie knows that no matter how difficult things may get during the chase, the brain-eating phase will make it all worth it. Remember also, that no zombie has ever eaten a brain or two, but then decided all the fuss wasn't really worth it. No zombie has retired to a solitary life of cats, X-Box, and/or daytime TV.

In your own life, you may have loved once or twice before, and found that love not to be lasting. You may have endured all-night shouting matches, breakups that splinter groups of friends, and alimony payments that never end. I'm not saying these things don't suck. They do. They really, really do. But remember the zombie.

Even if the last brain it munched wasn't the tastiest, there's no hesitation to get right back on the horse. A zombie keeps after what it wants. It knows that true love (brains) is out there.

The first step, then, to loving like a zombie, is to banish forever all doubts that true love is out there, and worth the hassle of courtship.

If you keep mementos of failed relationships around your home, throw them out. You don't need that souvenir tote that reminds you of the time he took you to the Grand Canyon, if it's only going to lead you down the slippery slope of wondering why he also cheated on you with your best friend, and if all men are like that, and if really you should just try to be happy on your own. That, my friend, is loser-talk. And zombies only talk like winners (when they talk at all).

Photos of exes, likewise, have got to go. I don't care if there are other people in the photos. If they're saved on your computer, just use the "delete" function, or at least Photoshop out the offending person.

If you're forever carrying around *memento mori* of bad relationships, you're not going to be motivated to get on to the next one. Trust me, picking through your scrapbooks this week may be a hassle, but when *amore* comes a-knockin', you'll be glad you did.

Are the offending items erased and waiting in a plastic bag out on the curb? Very good, we'll continue.

The next romance myth that zombies shatter is the one that insists that nobody would love you for you.

From the smallest dab of makeup to cover a blemish to the most elaborate exaggeration of one's wealth, status, and penis size, the quest for love often involves prevarication and deception. Why? Because we feel (erroneously) that we are somehow not good enough. So we lie, sometimes directly and sometimes indirectly.

We know full well that, if things go well, our partner will eventually notice that we do, in fact, get pimples when we're stressed. Or that we're not really titled shipping magnates who play billiards with George Clooney and Brad Pitt on the weekends, and that we pack it downstairs. We know this will make our partners feel deceived and confused, and may very well plant the seeds for a break-up. It makes no sense to lie like this, but we do it out of a feeling that we're not "good enough" as we are, and that it's the "only way" someone would fall in love with us.

You never see zombies lying or prevaricating because they don't feel "worthy" of someone's brain. Doesn't make much sense, does it? A zombie knows he (or she) is good enough just as God (or the voodoo priest, or the nerve reagent) made him. A zombie says, "Here I am. I can only be myself. Take me as I am. Give me your brain. "

A zombie doesn't need a bank account full of money, a fancy Ivy-League degree, or a clean felony record to feel worthy of its heart's desire. A zombie presents itself openly for what it is. Sure, high-functioning zombies pass for human now and then, but there's always that moment when the elevator doors close and the zombie lets its real self shine through.

Be Open and Direct

A zombie requires neither sex nor money, but it certainly has needs. Zombies put their own needs first. In every situation. All the time.

Just as a policy of complete honesty with romantic partners can seem like a lousy idea at first (or at least a counterintuitive one), looking for love by putting your own needs first (and keeping them there) might seem to contravene the rules of dating no less deeply.

Putting your needs first is, however, directly connected to a policy of honesty and openness in the quest to love like a zombie.

When a zombie wants to eat somebody, he will make that clear. He's not stopping to consider that person's needs. Or the needs of his/her friends and family. Or even the needs of other zombies who may also be advancing towards the potential victim.

Part of a zombie's refreshing openness is its way of acting in a manner that says: "It's great and all that you're 'too young to die.' And that you 'need' to go on living. But right now, it's not about you. Right now, this is about what I want. I have a right to my feelings, and I 'feel' like I'd like to eat your brain. This is who I am. I never claimed to be anything else. I'm sorry if you thought otherwise."

Zombie Tip:
You never get a second chance to make a first impression.

Zombies know they only have one shot to give people the correct impression. (That impression being that they're about to get eaten. Cause, you know, they are.)

See? What a gentleman.

A zombie knows inherently that it'd never get anywhere if it stopped to take into account all the feelings and desires of others that might conflict with its own.

A zombie wants to move a step closer to brains just like you want to move a step closer to true love. If that's something that somebody else can't get on board with, then it's their problem, not yours.

Be dogged, dog

Another way in which lovers can learn from zombies is in a zombie's pure doggedness and endless patience. When a zombie wants someone, it stays on the scent. It doesn't take "I already have a drink" or "my boyfriend will be right back" or "this shotgun is filled with rocksalt, you stinking zombie" as an answer.

And while **unreasonable** romantic doggedness can result in restraining orders or even jail time (and is, therefore, not suggested), there's no harm in asking someone out a second or third time. If at first you don't succeed, think of a new approach.

Zombies know that there's more than one way inside a fortified farm house. Sewers and storm drains can be opened. Gambrel roofs can be scaled, especially when you have all night. If all else fails, a zombie can go a lot longer than a human without eating. Many a zombie has starved a victim out of his or her fortification, and while waiting around is never fun, there's nothing else a zombie's got going on.

When there's someone you want to go out with, and for whatever reason the stars aren't right, remember the dogged patient zombie.

Your target may already be in a relationship. He or she may be physically removed from your part of the country. You may even have been rebuffed by him or her directly. Dear friend, all hope need not be lost.

Relationships end, and people go back on the market. People move back to their hometowns after a couple of years off "finding themselves" in the big city. People who once wouldn't return your calls may lower their standards as time goes by.

If you really want to find true love, you have to be open to the possibility that it could involve some waiting. But while you wait, wait like the zombie outside the fortified farmhouse.

The waiting zombie usually stays visible.

If the farmer screws up his courage and peeks through a crack in the door he's nailed shut, the zombie will be right outside waiting. If the object of your affection is dating someone else, let them know that, if they ever get bored with Mr. Whatsisname, you'll be right there, waiting to offer love, intimacy, and long, sloppy fellatio sessions.

When you can't be directly visible to the object of your affection, it's important to find other ways to let your presence be known. The zombie might not be right outside the farmhouse's front door anymore, but the creaking footsteps on the roof let the farmer know he's still the center of the zombie's world. You might not be able to stay physically near that gorgeous girl from college who said you'd never make anything of yourself, but your note to the alumni magazine about your JD from Harvard will let her know you're still out to prove her wrong.

It's important to note that only you can decide whether waiting is the right thing to do. Even zombies have to make tricky calls in this connection. Yes, a zombie will wait all week for an isolated farmer to risk venturing outside, but if there's another, un-fortified farmhouse just over the next hill, a zombie is no less of a zombie for going in search of other prey.

Go where the action is

The final lesson zombies embody for those desperately seeking someone, is to seek out a target-rich environment. It might sound a little inelegant for a chapter on finding true romance, but trust me, it is advice you need to take.

Have you ever noticed that when zombie outbreaks occur, they invariably start in cities? You've seen it before. One city falls, then another, as zombies radiate out from them. Humans who survive the zombies longest are the ones living in the flyover.

What attracts zombies to urban centers? The number of people-per-square-mile, of course. Cities are where zombies have the best chance of finding what they're looking for, and they instinctually know it. That's not to say that there might not be some very tasty brains in rural Montana or the Mojave Desert. Probably there are. But a zombie knows its best chance of finding brains to eat will be where people are packed as tight as they can be (and paying through the nose for it, no less).

Now before you go into a diatribe about how not everyone can live in a big city and how there are many positive aspects to a rural existence, hear this loud and clear: I am not

suggesting that you must live in a city to find love. At least, not necessarily . . .

What I am suggesting is that you do need to look for the kind of person you want to meet in the kind of place where that person lives. This doesn't automatically mean you need to pick up stakes, but you should consider the benefits of focusing your efforts on a target-rich-environment.

If you're idea of an ideal mate is someone who works in publishing, television, or art auctioneering, someone who likes to dress in black, and someone who enjoys live theater, then yes, you may be heading off for the Big Apple. But there are plenty of other qualities worth seeking. Your list may be very general (liberal or conservative, introverted or extroverted, outgoing or a homebody), or painstakingly specific (I want to meet an Orthodox Jewish dentist who enjoys Indian food and reads Saul Bellow). Whatever the case, you need to begin by asking yourself, honestly, where you are likely to find these types. Otherwise, you're just wasting your time. Frequently, just the smallest adjustment can yield results to make any zombie proud.

If you've always wanted to date a cop, but you spend your evenings in a bar where criminals congregate, your chances of meeting a handsome young police officer are pretty limited (at least, an off-duty one). If, on the other hand, you try the cop bar by the police station, your chances of success increase greatly.

If you want to meet a reader, go to the bookstore. (If you want to meet a broke-ass reader, try the library).

Someone athletic, hit the gym.

Many of us might like to imagine that someone who's a perfect match for us will just fall into our laps one day, or ride up on a white horse. But when you get tired of waiting, make like a zombie and go to where the targets are. You'll be glad you did.

To Recap:

Zombies know the catch is well worth the chase.

Zombies are up front about who they are, and what they need.

Zombies are dogged in their pursuit.

Zombies stick to a target-rich-environment.

To prepare for your next romantic encounter, whenever it happens, you need to prep yourself for the world of dating as a zombie.

Perfection Is a Skinned Knee

To be like a zombie, you must strive for perfection only in the most vital areas of (after)life. Even then, you must do so cautiously.

More than one self-help tome before this has insinuated that perfection is not possible, and that it's a dangerous standard for which to strive. These books are on the right track, more or less, but fail to tell the entire story when it comes to zombies. For a zombie, perfection is a little different from what it might be for you or me.

Perfection for a zombie?
Eating a human brain. Any brain.

Marvel, for a moment dear reader, at the zombie's ability to find perfection in such a simple and accessible thing. Brains are everywhere. People with brains are readily accessible **to** zombies. The dream can be realized again and again.

When humans speak of perfection, it is more frequently done in reference to the execution of a project (usually, a project that can be quantified in some way).

"I got a perfect 1600 on my SAT."

"He pitched a perfect game last season."

"I got a perfect score on Centipede."

Things that are not quantifiable or score-able are likewise spoken of as being less-than-perfect.

"No marriage can be perfect, but I never expected to fight this much."

"Some people dream of a perfect life, but not me."

"A graduate of Eton is expected to be perfect in his comportment, and not go to Halloween parties dressed as a Nazi."

Zombie Tip:
I have taken more from brains . . .

than brains have taken from me.

Seriously, brains are awesome. Have we made that clear yet?

This tends to imply a kind of double-standard when it comes to perfection. Humans create situations for themselves where perfection is measurable and quantifiable, when really, who's to say what's perfect?

Here we begin to see the paradox of perfection that zombies have long ago figured out:

By focusing on perfection, humans make their lives imperfect.

By never worrying about doing things perfectly, zombies experience perfect happiness.

As remarked, many self-help authors have opined that an obsession with perfection does not lead to happiness. Zombies have discovered that the opposite is also true. By never worrying about whether or not you've gotten something perfect, you tend to experience a rollicking happiness that is, well, pretty darn perfect.

For instance, when a zombie's making his way through a day care center during a power outage, he doesn't worry about whether or not he's going to eat the brain of **every** child inside. When a zombie is locked in a to-the-death (or "death") combat with a human, he doesn't stop to worry about things going perfectly. If he's got to smash his victim's head on a rock, precious and delicious brains could be lost. If he

decapitates the human in a wet or muddy battlefield, the brains could get all gooey and gross. (And who wants to eat a muddy brain? Totally gross, am I right?) Numerous things can "go wrong" in the course of combat. Does this stop the zombie? Not for a second. Win or lose, partial-muddy-brain or delicious-entire-brain, the zombie is just going for it like he always does. Nine times out of ten, the zombie finds that things go great when he just goes for it like that.

Your exercise for the rest of this week will involve training yourself to "just stumble in wildly" like a zombie, and not worry about perfection. In your journal, make note of each occasion when you feel yourself making an appeal towards perfection, note the way in which you instead adopt a zombie's more freestyle perfection approach, and note the end result of the situation. Dollars-to-delicious-yummy-brains, I'll bet you that most of the time, taking on a zombie's less obsessive stagger ends with an imminently more perfect result.

Here are some examples:

Example One

Situation demanding perfection: Have to do a sales presentation at the distributors' convention in Skokie. If we don't get picked up by at least as many outlets as last year, this mom and pop business of ours it pretty much shot. My initial impression is that my pitch with these guys has got to be perfect, and I should do a lot of drafts, and stay up all night practicing. Maybe even hire an outside speechwriter.

Revised zombie approach: Okay, so I thought about my zombie training up to this point in the book, and I thought, a zombie would just go for it, right? A zombie would just do what it wanted to do. Charge right in. Just be itself. So I didn't come up with a fancy pitch or hire a speechwriter. (I did stay up all night, but at a bar.) Then, at the convention, I just walked right up to the distributors, even if they were already talking to somebody else, and I was like: "I've clearly got the best products and selection, and at prices you can't beat. You'd be brainless not to stock our products."

End result: Maybe the zombie-training inspired me to use the word "brainless," but whatever the case, it was just what these guys needed to hear. We filled all the orders we needed, and then some. This is one mom and pop sex toy and pornography manufacturer that's going to be okay!

Example Two

Situation demanding perfection: Coach gives me a lecture after last game about how left guard is one of the most important positions on the offensive line, and says that if I keep giving up so many sacks, I stand to lose my scholarship. (Can he **do** that?) Anyhow, I felt right away like I'd better play perfect for the rest of the season. For a moment, I saw myself hitting the weight room more, not skipping

Sunday practices, and maybe using protein shakes to bulk up like I've seen some of the other guys do.

Revised zombie approach: Anyhow, so right as the coach sat back down and said "Is that clear, son? Now get out of my office!" I started thinking that I should try to be perfect like a zombie would, and not like a human. I was like, a zombie wouldn't care if it started, or if it got playing time. It would only go after what it wanted. In **this** situation, I want my scholarship just like a zombie wants brains. I don't need a perfect or elegant way of getting it, so I said: "Coach, I'd like to try harder for you and all that bullshit, but I'm afraid that if I do, I'll go to the dean of students and tell him about all those times I let you suck my cock. Like here, just now, in this office with your door closed like it is. Now look, you can bench me if you don't like Terry getting sacked nine times a game. That's fine. But if my scholarship goes, then I gotta be real with the top brass about all those times you begged me to run a triple-reverse slant route into your ass."

End result: Scholarship secure.

Whatever the situation, send perfection packing and embark instead with the unconcerned spirit of a zombie. When you do, you'll find yourself as close to "perfection" as one is likely to come, and you find had a fun time getting there!

Week

9

No Credit
Letting Go of Your Ego and Adopting a Zombie's Spirit of Cooperation

Too many humans today are motivated to act only when and if their actions will result in some sort of credit. They want their actions to be recorded. How often have you heard:

> *"Sure I'm interested in helping, but I want my name attached to the project."*
>
> -or-
>
> *"Will the press be there? Because otherwise it's not even worth showing up."*
>
> -or-
>
> *"I'll only be an extra in this film if I can appear in the credits as 'Zombie #281.'"*

The attitude evinced in these examples is completely antithetical to that of the zombie, who is completely unconcerned with being credited for his actions (and in many cases would much prefer to be left out of any sort of record entirely).

The purpose of week 9 is to inspire you to slough off this all-too-human preoccupation with credit and embrace a more zombie-like way of being.

Previous sections of this book have already commented extensively upon the zombie's comportment. Specifically, it has been stressed that zombies don't do what they do out of any need for external attention. In this section, we note that neither are zombies concerned with being credited for their work. If Zombie A breaks down a door and eats someone's brain, but then history should mistakenly credit Zombie B with this act, nobody involved is very concerned. Not Zombie A. Not Zombie B. Nobody.

Zombies are creatures free from the constraints of Ego (and Id and Superego, while we're at it). They do what they do only because they want to do it, and not for any exterior acknowledgment or hope for a place in history.

Zombie Tip:
Meditate about it!

The ancient practice of clearing one's mind by sitting quietly focusing on one's breathing was tailor-made for zombies. Zombies already sit quietly most of the time, and focus on brains only because they do not breathe. This lived-state of near constant meditation indicates a zombie's close proximity to nirvana.

In fact, when something mysterious is conspicuously un-credited, there is all the more reason to believe that zombies were involved.

Let us drive home the point. While some historical events have seemed mysterious and confusing to present day historians, the influence of uncredited zombies is readily detectable in the following:

Construction of Stonehenge in Ancient England

While no one knows exactly who the Druids were (or what they were doin'), ancient British zombies were prescient enough to understand that building a confusing stone obelisk would be enough to bring edible humans to an otherwise empty stretch of land. (This, being before cities existed in northern England, was actually less effort than trekking down to London.) To this day, the odd tourist is lost to the zombies who still frequent the spot.

Construction of the Pyramids in Ancient Egypt

Though some historians still profess to be "baffled" at how ancient man could have had the sufficient technology, motivation, and endurance to create these monuments to the dead (clue), more open-minded anthropologists have long understood that the implementation of zombie-labor could be an important missing ingredient. (This was, of course, prior to the great Zombie–Mummy rift, when it became apparent to all that mummies were just unambitious rich kids who wanted to play in their enormous houses but never wanted to come outside and try actually **working** for a living.)

Destruction of the Knights Templar

Saracen invaders and Papal conspiracies tend to dominate modern theories as to the extinction of this ancient order, but few know that the "Knights of Malta" actually retreated to their island as a defense against zombies more than anything else. (This defense was not effective.)

Disappearance of Amelia Earhart

Stowaway zombie.

Loss of Ocean Liner "Titanic"

Stowaway zomb*ies* (navigator eaten).

In this connection, it is important to note that there are no individually famous zombies. At least no **openly** famous zombies. Think about that for a second . . .

Zombies, **as a species**, are famous for lots and lots of things, and have obviously accomplished quite a bit. But you never see a single zombie singled-out for fame.

When a zombie is successful and receives attention, he

doesn't let the media single him out as anything more than "a zombie." Not "Bill Taylor the former tax attorney turned Zombie," not "Bill the Zombie," and not even "that one zombie in the Brooks Brothers suit from 1972 with half its jaw missing."

The only credit a zombie will accept is when he is credited simply as "a zombie."

Rather than garnering personal attention, a zombie prefers to be a credit only to his race . . . the zombie race.

So the next time you have a chance to tack your name onto a work project (that you really didn't help with that much), get a "Based on Characters Created By" screenwriting credit (when all you really did was say "Hey . . . what if there's also a talking dog or something?" one time at a read-through), or discover a secret nerve toxin that can turn deceased human cadavers into the walking dead, remember:

A zombie never asks to be credited for his work, because the work itself should be its own reward.

Week

10

Do Go There
(and Stay There Until You Get What You Want)

As we enter the final stretch of your zombification training, it's time to focus on a final lesson about interacting with others. Namely, the places zombies can take you and the places they take other people.

There is virtually no place that a zombie will not go, physically or otherwise. In previous sections we've focused on how this endows it with such obvious traits as fearlessness and bravery. A zombie's willingness to "go" anywhere is another thing that makes it an excellent model.

The oft repeated admonition "Don't **go** there" is already suspect. After evolving naturally in the vernacular, these days it tends to be relegated to sarcastic and ironic uses. In the media, it tends only to be used by ethnic sitcom characters. As flummoxing and nonsensical as the expression might be for you or me, it has even less meaning for a zombie. A zombie takes orders and advice from no one, and certainly doesn't hesitate to go somewhere that has brains to eat.

In the world of the average human, warnings against "going there" tend to relate not to physical places as much as levels of discourse. Sure, now and then you'll hear something like:

> *"The Tool Box? Don't go* **there** *on a weekend. It's* **such** *a meat-market."*
>
> -or-
>
> *"Don't go* **there** *for your next suit. Let my uncle save you a bundle at his store instead."*

But more frequently, it's:

> *"Don't* **go there***, girlfriend. My man is off limits."*
>
> -or-
>
> *"Don't* **go there** *before five o'clock. That kind of talk can make for sexual harassment charges."*
>
> -or-
>
> *"Don't* **go there***. He's really sensitive about it!"*

When we are admonished, as in these later examples, it is not against physically going to a particular place or location. Rather, it is a topic, subject, or field of study that is not allowed.

Succinctly, the zombification lesson for week 10 is to always, always ignore such urgings.

Remember:

Zombies go wherever they want, and this makes them successful.

To be like a zombie, go wherever you want, physically or otherwise.

Not "going there" might sound like good advice, and many times the people giving it to you can be well-meaning. However, as a zombie, you should **always** go there. You should go there without evening thinking about it. It should, and will, become second nature.

Our first exercise this week will illustrate the value of such a policy. Take up your pen and make a list of at least three examples that stick out in your mind of times when you **didn't** go there. It can be somewhere physical as well as somewhere figurative, but be sure to include the topical going there too. Make sure you describe the situation and what your goal was, your interaction or action, the place you didn't "go," and the short and long term result. Be as detailed as you need to be.

Your finished list might look like this:

Setting: Bill and I are both up for the promotion to Regional VP. Ms. Fleming calls both of us into her office at the same time to talk about the Beta 3 project.

Goal: Get the promotion. Bill and I both worked on Beta 3, so obviously the boss is just trying to tell which one of us was the real brains behind the project that made it work.

Interaction: Fleming talks to me first, which is good because I can talk about all the work I did with the business model and cross-selling the functionality. I lay it all out and I'm totally honest. I figure this is a good way to go, since I really did 90 percent of the work on Beta 3, and Bill mostly suggested things that didn't work and then took a vacation. I don't want to be snitty though, so I just mention that Bill was away for a little of it.

Then Bill gets his turn and goes into this ridiculous spiel where he doesn't even mention Beta 3. Instead, he just starts lying through his teeth. He talks about how he was on vacation for part of the project because he was going to India to meditate with a guru in a zero carbon-impact Sakra center, or something. He concludes by saying how the trip gave him this special insight into what Beta 3 needed to work, and how his input saved the project.

Laughable, right?

The problem is, Fleming is into Yoga and meditation and stuff (there is a fucking dreamcatcher hanging above her desk for chrissake) and she's eating this up hand over fist. Also at issue, in my opinion, is the fact that Bill didn't go to India. He went to *Indiana,* specifically to spend his bonus on riverboat gambling, Chivas, and full-contact lap dances.

Where I didn't go: I wanted to tell Fleming the truth about Bill, but it felt like a low blow. (Also, isn't there supposed to be a rule that what happens in Hammond stays in Hammond?) I was confused about how to proceed, and I just kept my mouth shut and hoped Fleming would see through it.

Result: As Regional VP, Bill has twice as much money and vacation time to Hoosier-away, and I have a new dreamcatcher hanging over my desk.

Setting: Running for Alderman in Chicago. Incumbent is a loveable icon and neighborhood fixture. He's also in bed with zoning board, taking kickbacks from everybody, and three of the five "elevator inspectors" he appointed to the city payroll are relatives who have never been seen actually inspecting an elevator.

Goal: Beat this guy.

Interaction: I get my campaign off the ground—really grass roots, my family and friends and stuff—and then there's this article in the *Sun-Times* about how I want to run as a reformer and am all excited about the debate coming up. Suddenly, this group of business leaders and local clergy want to meet with me. I'm thinking, "Score! These people are ready for real change."

But when I arrive, they're all: "Our current alderman is a pillar of the community. He gets things done. People know him and love him. Children wave to him in the park." Like this guy is Santa Claus or something.

So I say, "Look, everybody knows he takes dirty money and gives his relatives jobs they don't do. I know he gets things done, but I can get things done too."

And they say: "Our alderman has the complete support of our chamber of commerce and the interfaith alliance. We're not telling you not to run, but those things 'everybody knows' have never been proved. You bring them up at the debate, and there're gonna be consequences. Maybe we find some things in your past, too."

And I'm thinking, do they know about the thing in my fraternity with the sheep?

Where I didn't go: The debate rolls around and like a dumbass I stick to topics like parking stickers, building a new playground in Madlangbayan Park, and starting neighborhood watch programs.

Result: He hands me my ass on election day. I go back to being a deputy clerk in Streets and Sanitation.

Do the above examples look a little like yours? If they do, don't feel bad. It's a challenge to take the fight where it needs to go. We're taught from childhood not to "make waves" or "be mean to people." We opt out of things because we have accepted the lie that some things are off limits "because they just are." Consequently, we allow ourselves to get talked out of doing the very things we want to do (and saying the things we want to say). Pointing out that a beloved man is a crook, or that a failed man is (on top of it all) also stupid, gives us a twinge of guilt.

It shouldn't.

Zombies feel no guilt. Or shame. They just take the fight to the enemy as hard as they can.

Some people think of "going there" as fighting dirty or using unnecessary force.

Did you ever hear of a zombie who wanted a good, clean fight? Do zombies spare the feelings (physical and emotional) of certain parties out of mercy and decorum? Do you ever hear of zombies making a "clean kill" with pistols at dawn, or whatever?

No, no, and no.

Zombies just fight to get what they want. There is no measure of force which they hesitate to expend toward their end. When attacked, zombies react like Clinton political campaigns. When on the attack, zombies use everything in their arsenal.

History books aren't going to censure zombies for using superior force against an obviously inferior foe. (And certainly not for insinuating that Barack Obama had slaveowning ancestors.)

Therein lies the lesson.

When you become like a zombie, you will assume a zombie's don't-fuck-with-me reputation. Those who consider attacking you will understand that doing so would mean total war. No skirmishes. No calculated strikes on military installations only. Only complete life-or-death combat until one of you has lost his or her brain.

> **Zombie Tip:**
> **Your eyes SHOULD be bigger than your stomach.**
>
> The concept of overeating is utterly nonsensical to a zombie. So don't sweat it if this is your third helping and your buffet plate is so overloaded and piled high that everyone turns to gape. To have seconds, or thirds, or thirty-fifths, is very like a zombie.

There are numerous advantages to attaining this reputation. No one messes with you lightly. There is no gangstering, steering, or intimidation. Those who do want to fight you to the death will do so, and they won't pussyfoot around beforehand, either.

For the rest of week 10, you will live out this maxim by adopting a zombie's tactic of "going there" as completely as possible, and in every situation.

In your day-to-day interactions this week, do your best to notice when someone is giving you a "don't go there" kind of message. It could be as obvious as a construction worker asking you to detour your walk because of freshly lain pavement, or as subtle as a batted eyelash and a disapproving glance at a cocktail party. When you think it may be happening, ask yourself how you might ignore the suggested on the grandest possible scale. Just like a zombie.

A referee's giant gut and patchy beard might be "off limits" to the other parents at the Little League game, but you need to start calling him Paunchy McPeachfuzz if you want your kid's strike zone to get any bigger.

The rest of the family might make a point not to rent *Roxanne* around your long-nosed sister-in-law. But you like Steve Martin, so go for it, dude. Hell, bring up the similarities if you need to. It should be plain as, you know . . .

A work superior's ovoid shape might be a well-known point of sensitivity, but you need to remember names, especially during the first month, and "eggman" is so much easier than "president and founder."

Keep it up, and you'll soon enjoy the results in many areas.

Aside from the occasional fight to the death, people interacting with you will adopt a much more pleasant and effective demeanor towards you, knowing full well that every physical flaw, emotional failing, and recurring venereal condition is fair fodder for your arsenal. In fact, the catapults are already loaded and aimed.

When the world knows you will "go there" with alacrity and ease, your life will go much easier.

And for the people who just met you, well, aren't **they** in for a surprise?

In the Zombie Zone

There are many paths toward success, and many ways to move forward. The self-help sections of bookstores offer a panoply of choices. You can live your "best life" by affirming what's important to you, utilize "the secret" of focusing on something you want all goddamn day, or even "stop using psychoactive drugs" if that's your thing.

One of the important differences, however, between this book and others like it, is that by becoming like a zombie, the traits and good habits you adopt will become second nature. We repeat them week-by-week in this part of the book so that you can add them one at a time, until they become as automatic as reacting. A zombie doesn't walk around thinking "be like a zombie . . . be like a zombie . . . " or "what would a zombie do in this situation?" A zombie just does. It just is.

If you've made it as far as week 11, and I hope you have (there is nothing more pitiful than a zombie-drop out), then you've already seen the positive impact that becoming more like a zombie has on your life. I'd like to applaud your persistence, because getting this far has required some effort. As you prepare for complete zombihood, there is one last thing we are going to change.

Let me start by asking some questions:

Have you ever had a really good day when everything seemed to go right?

Have you ever been in a place where you were able to make all the right decisions automatically, without hesitating or second-guessing yourself?

Have you ever been, as the sportscasters say, in the zone?

It's normal to have occasional moments of greatness in which we don't make any errors—in which we simply know exactly what must be done and then do it. Everyone occasionally experiences something like this. The trick is finding a way back to these moments, which are as mysteri-

---

 Zombie Tip: Make time for yourself.

With today's hectic, modern schedules, it's important for us to find ways to make times for the activities we really value. Whether it's more time with the kids, "private lessons" with your tennis instructor Hans, or eating a bunch of people, you've got to make "me" time. Nobody else is going to do it for you.

ous and fleeting as they are invigorating and wonderful. The way is difficult, however, and far too many stand to profit from providing bad advice.

Since the earliest snake-oil salesmen, consumers have proved ready and willing to buy any and every product that promised a way back to being in "the zone." Whether it's repressed-memory psychotherapy, a new fad diet, or a heavily advertised sugared sports drink, these routes to effectiveness often prove to be no more than an expensive distraction.

Especially when it comes to the self-help model, those seeking enlightenment exhibit a broad insatiability that, at least theoretically, should not exist if the books are doing what they all promise to do. Yet the self-help pantheon is full of authors who are read concurrently, and even recommend one another to the reader. If one author's "Guide to Happiness and Fulfillment" actually works, then the reader should have no use for subsequent releases like *The Companion to Happiness*, *Happiness 101* and, of course, *The Zen of Happiness and Fulfillment.* Doubtless, the true seeker of self mastery will eventually notice this contradiction, but only after a substantial investment of time and money.

The quest for self-knowledge and effectiveness is not a bootless one, however. And many current self-help gurus have got a thing or two right (taking, as they do, stab after stab after stab). Their flaw has merely been to look in the wrong place for a model.

Consider:

Who feels "in the zone" all the time?
Who never hesitates or doubts himself?
Who always know what to do next?
For whom is every day a "good" day?

Answer: A zombie.

In charting the path to self-knowledge, too many authors have made the error of the pathetic fallacy. That is to say, they have assumed that the outside of something must reflect what the inside is like. That people's bodies reflect their souls. That a dirty, rotten, but nonetheless animated, corpse has nothing to tell the world about a vibrant inner-life.

Yet counterexamples abound.

Physically ugly people often have very beautiful souls and are wonderful on the inside. Beautiful and handsome people can prove to be morally ugly and spiritually spoiled. Zombies, who frequently induce vomiting on sight (or smell), are the most important creatures of all when you need a spiritual guide.

Other self-help authors often encourage their readers to adopt physical fitness regimes under the misguided notion that they will "feel good about themselves when they feel good about their bodies." Zombies have bodies that are decomposing and broken, yet nobody feels better than a zombie.

Other gurus suggest you "make time for yourself" so you don't get "burned out" by life. Zombies see that when you know what you want, its relentless pursuit is not a burden but a pleasure of incredible magnitude.

The same authors urge their readers to "find a balance" between "work, home, finances, and love." Zombies are so well balanced that they don't even understand the idea of being imbalanced by their pursuits.

In every avenue in which it is possible to do so, zombies have demonstrated the actuality of a self-help reader's dream. They don't hesitate, and they feel in the zone all the time. They don't worry. They don't tire. They don't get intimidated. They always know what to do.

But, let's be frank . . . they look like hell. (It isn't intentional, but it's there.)

In our superficial society, it is apparent that even the top minds in self-help have winced at the idea that anything that looked so bad could be so good.

Dressing up (or down) as a zombie will not make you like a zombie on the inside. However, becoming like a zombie internally may lead to the adoption of some exterior zombie-traits. This should not concern or alarm you. After all, it is some of our best minds who most frequently fall short in the appearance department. One has only to remember Einstein's general disheveledness, Godel's inability to match shirt with tie, or Edmund Husserl's penchant for going days without a bath, to understand that great thinking goes along with zombie-like tendencies.

As the zombie lessons of this book sink in and become more and more second nature to you, don't be alarmed if you see slight external changes taking place. As you concentrate on life's important aspects, vanities like makeup, hairspray, and deodorant are likely to slip your mind. Your unerring focus on your prize may override entirely your eye's reflex to blink, giving you a zombie's thousand-yard stare. Your greatly economized zombie-speech may result in crust around your mouth from lack of use.

These are badges of honor, to be worn accordingly.

Getting in the zombie-zone is one thing. Making it your default setting is another. By this point, you're probably "on" most of the time. Still, there can be situations and circumstances that occasionally jar you right out of zombie mode.

Your exercise this week will involve keeping a record of things that threw you, and making notes about how to deal with them going forward.

A dieter may inexplicably fail week after week, until one day he notices that his regular Sunday stroll takes him past a cake shop. Charting a new route for his weekend saunter will likely save his waistline.

In that connection, the things that throw you out of the zombie zone, and leave you doing and saying things that aren't very zombie-like at all, can usually be successfully countered once they are isolated. It may feel that you are sometimes just randomly moved to less-than-zombie-like behavior. However, a week of observant monitoring usually allows you to identify a cause. Steps can then be taken towards correction.

Whenever you feel yourself falling out of the zombie zone this week, stop and write it down. Note the situation, what showed that you had been jarred, and what the factors might have been. It may not happen each day. Conversely, it may happen frequently, in which case you should write down the most memorable instances.

By the end of the week, your list should look something like this:

Example One

Situation: It's crowded today on the bus. I'm minding my own business in the back like a zombie. This one woman next to me has all these packages under her arm, a handbag, and is carrying a baby to boot. The driver takes a corner a little too fast, and suddenly she loses her balance and starts going over.

Manifestation: Before I know what I'm doing, I reach over and help. Her packages go everywhere, but she stays upright and the kid's okay. At the next stop, I help her pick up the packages. Then I sit back down. Would a zombie do this? It doesn't feel right.

Possible cause: Child in peril?

Example Two

Situation: Driving from work to my daughter's recital today, this jerk rear ends me. Not too hard, but I didn't see it coming and was totally shocked. I don't feel like a zombie anymore. It's like the collision has knocked it out of me.

Manifestation: I get out and we swap insurance. The damage isn't bad, and the guy says he's sorry and everything, but still, I can't shake the feeling that I should have attacked the guy and eaten his brains.

Possible cause: Auto collision?

Example Three

Situation: Music critic in the local paper gives my band's CD a bad review. Any press is good press, but I honestly thought he would like it, and I can't decide how a zombie should respond. Do I track him down and eat his brain? Then again, zombies treat everyone the same, and if some guy at a show says we suck, I'd crack his skull open and eat his brains for sure.

Manifestation: I just ignore it and don't say anything, but at practice I can tell that the guys have read it. We practiced like usual and everything, but they are pretty bummed.

Possible cause: Negative attention?

Now that you have compiled your own instances of going out of the zombie zone, see if the possible causes you identity are similar to the ones in the above examples. Notably, they all involve the unexpected. Each situation involves a surprise. Likely, none of the subjects have experienced these situations since beginning their zombification process.

Another thing I hope you'll have in common with the people in these examples is that, despite their concerns, they have all passed the test and responded in a zombie-appropriate way. (You don't always have to be **feeling like** a zombie to keep **acting like** one. If you feel you've been thrown out of your zone, trust your training to take over.)

Our bus-riding zombie acolyte doubts himself because he was helpful. Yet if he's a naturally helpful person, and his goal is helping people when he can, then this is one hundred percent consistent with being like a zombie. After the incident is concluded and the woman's things are restored, he lets it go and goes back to being an energy-conserving zombie. Looks pretty good to me.

Our automobile commuter feels he's done something wrong because his response is banal and pedestrian. He inspects the damage, swaps insurance, and receives an apology. This seems uninspired, but his goal is to get to his daughter's recital. Continuing on after the accident would likely cause him to get flagged down, or possibly reported for leaving the scene. Though the subject considers violence a more appropriate zombie response, it would only have distracted him from his ultimate goal. A way forward may be banal and uninteresting, but if it's also the most expeditious way, then it's what a zombie would take.

Our rock musician also stays true to his zombihood by staying on target. A zombie who's hot on the chase doesn't get distracted if someone writes "zombies suck" on a wall somewhere. He doesn't disengage the current target and go off to eat the brain of the graffiti artist. Our rocker doesn't get distracted from his dream of topping the charts just because one reviewer didn't like his work. He doesn't even miss a practice. Very like a zombie.

Granted, you may have some re-reading in store if your examples involve you screaming and crying like a small child. (Whatever the situation, zombies don't do that.) But a slight apparent diversion from your "zone" should not be cause for undue alarm.

So when in doubt, let your training up to this point take over and guide you. Trust yourself to react in a zombie-appropriate way to a situation, and chances are, you will!

Remember to stay on target.

The Zen of Zombie

How will you know when you've attained full zombihood? Will there be a signal from above like a thunderclap, or will the final change be a small one—barely perceptible even to yourself?

The answer to that question is different for each person. Yet as the exercises and lessons in this book become more and more like second nature, you will begin to come into your own as a zombie. Just as all zombies are not exactly alike, so too will disciples of the zombie find that they do not resemble one another point for point. Being a zombie is something you have to make your own. **In this final week, you job is to let the zombie training take over.**

Throughout history, prophets and seers have attempted to describe the experience of finally attaining nirvana or a zen-state. Their wording is often confusing though, and can run the gamut from the inane to the overly poetic. You read these accounts and you run into wording like:

*"I had the realization that I was the actuality of all things,
and that all things were the actuality of my reality."*
   -or-

*"I felt a oneness with the creator-god that flowed through
me and was outside of me and yet a part of me at the
same time."*
   -or-

*"The divine current of heavenly knowledge held me
down and penetrated me repeatedly. From behind."*

Prophets of the traditional routes to a state of zen usually speak in confusing poetic generalities like this because they have to. Their deliverables of "self-knowledge," "existential awareness," and "divine enlightenment" are highly suspect, and usually don't live up to people's expectations. (Note: If you have to ask "Did I just experience enlightenment? Was that it?" then get a new guru honey, because . . . Guess what? You didn't.) Or else they are presented as riddles, which, for our purposes, we may dispense with entirely. (Could a zombie eat a brain so tasty that he himself could not finish it?)

Zombie-zen, thankfully, is much more specific in its mani-

Zombie Tip:
When does a boy become a man? When he has to.

But when does a man become a zombie? Upon
the successful completion of this book, of course.

festations, and very easy to notice when you've attained it.
Descriptions usually run more along the lines of:

"I found myself in a never-ending nightmarish afterlife of
shreiking skinless gibberings for the goo inside of people's
heads."

While, again, every zombie is at least a little different from
other zombies, certain constants run through all who have
attained zombie-zen:

Your enemies tremble in fear when you approach

You never tremble in fear

**Those who oppose you understand that
the only form of "negotiation" you'll
entertain is a fight to the death.**

**You only speak when absolutely
necessary and when it furthers your goals**

You treat all people equally

**You don't hold grudges or keep vendettas
(which is not to say you can't be violent
generally . . . in fact, it is encouraged)**

**You keep your cool in all situations,
and make the best of all situations**

You don't have a big ego or need to be credited for your accomplishments

You are an agent of peace in the world (except when you're, you know, attacking somebody)

Like a zombie, you stay focused and always know exactly what to do

The attainment of zombie-zen may hit you all at once, or it may be gradual. You could be walking (like a zombie) down the street one day and think to yourself, "Hey, I just noticed that everything on that checklist is true about me!" But your zombie journey does not end with the completion of this book. Rather, it begins. The end of your time as a human is a new beginning of your life as a zombie. No one can tell you what kind of zombie you're going to be. You have to find that out for yourself.

Becoming a zombie is a unique experience that you'll be certain to enjoy. You'll notice improvements in all aspects of your life. Your gait may be a little choppier. Your clothing a little more tattered. Your speech slurred as a drunk's, certainly. But you'll also be happier, more effective, and more at peace than you've ever been before.

Zombie-zen is that inarticulable, mysterious sum-total of all that you have attained up to this point. And like so many transcendent experiences, the whole is greater than the sum of the parts. (Especially if those "parts" are parts of people you're having for lunch.

Zombie-zen is all about pushing your own thoughts and impulses aside and letting the zombie **inside** take control. (How do you know if he's in control? Are you running amok like a berzerker cannibal barbarian out of control? Then, yeah, he's probably holding the reins.)

Zombie-zen is a way of being, but it's also a "be" of weighing. That is to say, you should always "be weighing" the impact of your actions as they relate to a zombie's goals. Are you getting what you really want in a given situation? Weigh it carefully, and when the answer indicates otherwise, adjust your position accordingly.

Attaining zombie-zen calms the nagging questions and doubts in your mind. Did you ever hear the expression "peace of mind?" That's what they're talking about. Peace and quiet from your own pesky insecurities and concerns. When you've attained zombie-zen, you won't worry about things or wonder what to do. Gone will be the nights of lying awake in bed, tossing and turning endlessly over such trivialities as:

> *Did I take the garbage out?*
>   -or-
> *Does that bonus mean I have to file quarterly taxes—and how do I file quarterly taxes?*

-or-

Might it be morally questionable to eat another man's brain only to sate my own selfish hunger?

These concerns will pass like the insignificant gadflies they are once you attain zombie-zen.

Like the monks of old, enlightened zombies live a spartan life, but one that is nonetheless deeply rewarding. When you attain zombie-zen, you'll no longer focus on trying to eat specific brains. Rather, you'll slow down and focus your attention on the greater "big brain" that is the very essence of life itself. (That much said, you **will** continue to eat specific brains, especially if you're a zombie.)

They say that when the student is ready, the teacher will appear. But if an actual, "living" zombie were to appear right in front of you, you wouldn't be here right now reading this. You would be eaten. Thus, we must make some adjustments, and make do as we must.

Zombies do not teach us to attain their zen-like state through direct one-on-one instruction. Likewise, they do not (directly) author self-help books, open meditation clinics, or sell tickets to enthusiastic motivational lectures to be held at one of the hotels out by the airport. Instead, they teach us by example. A zombie's actions are his lessons (when the student has become properly attuned to seeing them).

A zombie's silence is his wisdom.

His moan is his koan.

His very way of being is his zen.

Endnote

While this book may be one of the first attempts to disperse the lessons to be taken from zombies to the general populace, it would not be correct to give the impression that the author is the first to make these observations. Many successful figures throughout history (as well as certain contemporary persons of note) have obviously taken some of the lessons of the zombie to heart, if not become zombies entirely.

To wit:

The late Gerald Ford is rumored to have been a zombie for the last several years of his "life."

The famously "soft-spoken" Calvin Coolidge was actually a very talkative zombie.

Terrifying 1960s film actor Tor Johnson was, of course, a zombie—though atypical in at least one important way. (Most humans *lose* weight when zombified . . .)

Anna Nicole Smith . . . Towards the end . . . Yeah . . .

Actor and Republican political strategist Ben Stein has built his entire career aping the diction and tone of a zombie.